CHINA'S HUMAN RIGHTS LAWYERS: CURRENT CHALLENGES AND PROSPECTS

ROUNDTABLE

BEFORE THE

CONGRESSIONAL-EXECUTIVE COMMISSION ON CHINA

ONE HUNDRED ELEVENTH CONGRESS

FIRST SESSION

JULY 10, 2009

Printed for the use of the Congressional-Executive Commission on China

Available via the World Wide Web: http://www.cecc.gov

U.S. GOVERNMENT PRINTING OFFICE

51–189 PDF   WASHINGTON : 2009

For sale by the Superintendent of Documents, U.S. Government Printing Office
Internet: bookstore.gpo.gov   Phone: toll free (866) 512–1800; DC area (202) 512–1800
Fax: (202) 512–2104   Mail: Stop IDCC, Washington, DC 20402–0001

CONTENTS

Page

Opening statement of Charlotte Oldham-Moore, Staff Director, Congressional-Executive Commission on China 1

Grob, Douglas, Cochairman's Senior Staff Member, Congressional-Executive Commission on China 1

Pitts, Hon. Joseph R., a U.S. Representative from Pennsylvania, Member, Congressional-Executive Commission on China 2

Cohen, Jerome A., Professor, New York University School of Law; Codirector, U.S.-Asia Law Institute; and Adjunct Senior Fellow for Asia Studies, Council on Foreign Relations 4

Turkel, Nury, Attorney with Kirstein & Young, PLLC 9

Feinerman, James V., Professor of Asian Legal Studies, Georgetown University Law Center, Codirector, Asian Law and Policy Studies Program 11

Fu, Bob (Xiqiu), Founder and President, ChinaAid Association (CAA) 16

APPENDIX

PREPARED STATEMENTS

Cohen, Jerome A 28

Feinerman, James V 31

Fu, Bob (Xiqiu) 39

SUBMISSIONS FOR THE RECORD

Final Compilation of Translated Lawyers' Statements, submitted by Bob (Xiqiu) Fu 41

CHINA'S HUMAN RIGHTS LAWYERS: CURRENT CHALLENGES AND PROSPECTS

FRIDAY, JULY 10, 2009

CONGRESSIONAL-EXECUTIVE
COMMISSION ON CHINA,
Washington, DC.

The roundtable was convened, pursuant to notice, at 10:02 a.m., in room 628, Dirksen Senate Office Building, Charlotte Oldham-Moore, Staff Director, presiding.

Also present: Representatives Joseph Pitts and David Wu.

Also present: Douglas Grob, Cochairman's Senior Staff Member and Kara Abramson.

OPENING STATEMENT OF CHARLOTTE OLDHAM-MOORE, STAFF DIRECTOR, CONGRESSIONAL-EXECUTIVE COMMISSION ON CHINA

Ms. OLDHAM-MOORE. We'll get started. We're going to be joined shortly by Congressman Pitts, who is a Commissioner.

STATEMENT OF DOUGLAS GROB, COCHAIRMAN'S SENIOR STAFF MEMBER, CONGRESSIONAL-EXECUTIVE COMMISSION ON CHINA

Mr. GROB. Thank you. Good morning, everybody. Welcome to the CECC's eighth roundtable this year.

Before we get started, I would just like to say, on behalf of the Chairman and Cochairman of the Commission, that we are deeply saddened by the recent reports of deaths and injuries in the Xinjiang Uyghur Autonomous Region of China, and express heart-felt sympathy to Uyghur and Han Chinese individuals, and all individuals and their families who have suffered.

We are delighted this morning to have a distinguished panel of experts to discuss China's Human Rights Lawyers: Current Challenges and Prospects. I would like to gratefully acknowledge the presence of Representative Joe Pitts. Thank you, Commissioner Pitts, for joining us here this morning.

At this roundtable our distinguished panel will discuss China's human rights lawyers and their role in advancing the rule of law in China. We will examine the relationship between these lawyers, the Chinese government, and the Communist Party, and explore why Chinese authorities recently have stripped some prominent rights lawyers of their lawyers' licenses. We will delve into documented incidents of increased harassment of human rights lawyers in China, and ask what the future now holds for them, and also ask what their treatment suggests about the development of the rule of law in China more generally.

I'd like just to share with you this month's issue of Chinese Lawyer magazine, which features a cover story on a leading criminal defense attorney at a major Chinese law firm, a firm that has hundreds of attorneys in four cities, now in its 16th year of operation. Just two decades ago, such a law firm would have been somewhat unimaginable, and represents an important development in many ways. So does China's revised Lawyers Law, which took effect last year, and which contains provisions aimed at combating some of the difficulties that criminal defense lawyers in China face in representing their clients. Some provisions of the Lawyers Law conflict with China's Criminal Procedure Law, but overall the revision of the Lawyers Law too, is an important step.

Yet at the same time, we gather here today to discuss Chinese authorities' failure to renew the professional licenses of some prominent lawyers who take on what the government deems to be politically sensitive cases. So, for those who see a threat to justice anywhere as a threat to justice everywhere, it's only natural to ask the question: What does this portend for the future of procedural law in China in general in areas beyond what is classically known as human rights law, and extending as far as to commercial law and other areas of civil law and criminal law in China?

And so I now would like to turn the floor over to Representative Pitts and ask if you have a statement or remarks to make.

STATEMENT OF HON. JOSEPH R. PITTS, A U.S. REPRESENTATIVE FROM THE STATE OF PENNSYLVANIA, MEMBER, CONGRESSIONAL-EXECUTIVE COMMISSION ON CHINA

Representative PITTS. Thank you. Thank you, Mr. Grob. I really appreciate your holding this important roundtable discussion.

I am disturbed by the recent reports regarding human rights lawyers in China. More than 18 lawyers, I'm told, who have been representing sensitive human rights cases have not been able to renew their law licenses, according to Human Rights Watch. This number is unprecedented. Some reports even indicate that lawyers have been arrested and beaten, in some cases even kidnapped, because of their involvement in human rights cases.

Human rights attorney Gao Zhisheng, a prominent lawyer who has worked on religious freedom cases, has been missing since February 4 of this year. Li Heping, another lawyer who has defended Christian house church leaders, and Gao Zhisheng have been among the lawyers to be denied renewal of their law licenses. I personally met with some of these lawyers, including Li Heping. I'm very concerned with the effects that this trend will have on the rule of law in China and the basic human rights of the people, the Chinese people.

In addition, law firms are being pressured to provide authorities with ammunition to deny the licenses of lawyers involved in these sensitive human rights cases. On May 28, the New York Times reported, "In some cases the law firms were told that they could avoid difficulties by giving the lawyers failing grades in their annual performance evaluation." At least three law firms have not been allowed to pass inspection because of lack of cooperation with the government. These actions are clearly intended to intimidate lawyers and law firms into not taking these sensitive human rights cases.

So I look forward to hearing from our distinguished roundtable witnesses, receiving their insights and recommendations on the steps that we in the Congress, the U.S. Government, should take to further support the fundamental rights of the Chinese people and the attorneys who are seeking to uphold their human rights. I would like to extend a special welcome to my good friend, Bob Fu, who I've worked with for many years, and thank him for his work and dedication on behalf of human rights and religious freedom in China.

Thank you, Mr. Grob. I yield back.

Ms. OLDHAM-MOORE. Thank you, Congressman Pitts. We're really grateful that you are here today.

I'm going to do a quick introduction of our extraordinary group of panelists today.

We must always begin with Professor Jerome Cohen, who is an American treasure. Professor Cohen is a leading American expert on Asian law, has been a professor at the New York University School of Law since 1990, where he is also the codirector of the U.S.-Asia Law Institute.

Mr. Cohen is also an Adjunct Senior Fellow for Asia Studies at the Council on Foreign Relations. Before retiring from a partnership at Paul, Weiss, Rivken, Wharton at the end of 2000, Mr. Cohen represented many companies and individuals in contract negotiations, as well as in dispute resolutions in various Asian countries. He writes a biweekly column for Hong Kong's South China Morning Post and Taiwan's China Times and is a frequent pro bono consultant in human rights and criminal justice cases relating to China and Taiwan.

Mr. Cohen formerly served as Jeremiah Smith Professor and Director of East Asian Legal Studies, and Associate Dean at Harvard Law School. He has published several books, including "The Criminal Process in the People's Republic of China: 1949–1963," "People's China and International Law," and "Contract Law of the People's Republic of China," and many articles on Chinese law, as well as a general book, "China Today," coauthored with his wife, Joan Liebold Cohen.

Today Mr. Cohen continues his research and writing on Asian law, specifically focusing on criminal justice reform, dispute resolution, human rights, and the role of international law.

Mr. Cohen also served in government, first as an Assistant U.S. Attorney in Washington, DC in the late 1950s, and then as a consultant to the U.S. Senate Committee on Foreign Relations. Mr. Cohen is a Phi Beta Kappa graduate of Yale College and a graduate of Yale Law School, where he was editor-in-chief of the Yale Law Journal. He was law secretary to Chief Justice Earl Warren of the U.S. Supreme Court in the 1955 term, and law secretary to Justice Felix Frankfurter of the Supreme Court in the 1956 term.

Next to Mr. Cohen is Mr. Nury Turkel, who is an attorney at Kirstein & Young. Mr. Turkel is an attorney there and his practice focuses on commercial and regulatory matters.

Prior to joining Kirstein & Young, Mr. Turkel managed a Washington-based nonprofit organization, the Uyghur-American Association, which works to promote democratic freedoms of Uyghur people in China and Central Asia. He has testified before the U.S. Congress and given many presentations, including at the U.S. Military Academy, the National Defense University, and Columbia University. He has also published many columns and op-eds.

To my right is Professor James Feinerman, who we are very fortunate to have with us today. Professor Feinerman joined the Georgetown University Law Center faculty as a visiting professor for the 1985–1986 academic year. Immediately after law school he studied in the People's Republic of China. Subsequently he joined the New York firm of Davis, Polk & Wordwell as a corporate associate.

During 1982–1983, Professor Feinerman was a Fulbright lecturer on law at Peking University. In 1986, he was a Fulbright researcher in Japan. In 1989, he was awarded a McArthur Foundation Fellowship to study China's practice of international law.

During the 1992–1993 academic year, he was a fellow at Woodrow Wilson International Center for Scholars. From 1993–1995, on leave from the Law Center, Professor Feinerman was the director of the Committee on Scholarly Communication with China. Professor Feinerman served as the editor-in-chief of the American Bar Association's China Law Reporter from 1986 to 1998. He spent spring 2006 as Fulbright senior distinguished lecturer at Tsinghua University Law School in Beijing. Professor Feinerman is the author of numerous journal articles and opinion pieces on the rule of law in China and has coauthored two books.

Finally, Mr. Bob Fu, president of the ChinaAid Association. He is one of the leading voices in the world for the persecuted church in China. He was born and raised in mainland China, and graduated from the School of International Relations, People's University in Beijing.

He was a pastor at a house church in Beijing until he and his wife, Heidi, were jailed for two months for illegal evangelism in 1996. They fled to the United States as religious refugees in 1997. Mr. Fu founded the China Aid Association in order to draw international attention to the Chinese Government's human rights violations against house church Christians. He is now a visiting professor in Religion and Philosophy at Oklahoma Wesleyan University, and a Ph.D. candidate at Westminster Theological Seminary in Philadelphia. He has written numerous pieces, including as a guest editor for the China Law and Government Journal by the University of California, Los Angeles.

Lots of information there. Let's get right to it. Professor Cohen, we'd be delighted to hear your statement.

STATEMENT OF JEROME A. COHEN, PROFESSOR, NEW YORK UNIVERSITY SCHOOL OF LAW; CODIRECTOR, U.S.-ASIA LAW INSTITUTE; AND ADJUNCT SENIOR FELLOW FOR ASIA STUDIES, COUNCIL ON FOREIGN RELATIONS

Mr. COHEN. Thank you very much. I want to thank Representative Pitts for coming here and showing such concern for the lawyers of China who are worried about human rights. I want to thank, of course, Ms. Oldham-Moore, Mr. Grob, and the staff for organizing this.

In 1977, a former student of mine, Victor Li, published a very interesting book called, "Law Without Lawyers." His thesis was, China has a distinctive political-legal culture, it's not one, as in Western countries or elsewhere, that requires a prominent role for lawyers, and the world should be open to recognizing China's distinctive characteristics.

Deng Xiaoping and company, soon after, took a different view. They resurrected the Soviet model that China had imported during its first decade of Communism. They modified the model for economic purposes, but they retained it for political-legal purposes. That included reliance on lawyers.

Of course, the reliance on lawyers that China soon demonstrated throughout the 1980s and 1990s had many virtues. One of the problems, however, was when it came to human rights matters, the lawyers were subjected to restraints, just as Soviet lawyers were. This has been a continuing problem.

I have a formal statement; some of you may have a copy. I'm not going to read it, but I thought I would try simply to summarize it in the time allotted.

The 2007 amendment to the Lawyers Law offered some greater hope to lawyers that they would be able to take part in criminal cases to a greater extent, and that they would have more autonomy in governing their own affairs.

It has been an improvement in some respects. In other respects, however, there is vague language in the law about state security, et cetera, that is easily subject to manipulation to use against lawyers. What we have found, although China has about 150,000 lawyers, only a very tiny minority have shown an active interest in human rights matters, and perhaps not more than 1 percent make human rights matters the bulk of their professional concerns. That is natural. Lawyers have to make a living.

The problem is, the human rights lawyers who are active have consistently run into difficulty from the Ministry of Justice that controls them and from the local lawyers associations that operate with the guidance and instruction of the Ministry of Justice.

That is why, in Beijing and Shenzhen, and a few other places, rights lawyers have tried to gain democratic control over the local lawyers' association. They have only made modest progress. If you're interested, there is a recent issue of China Rights Forum about the rule of law that is one of the sources for following the struggle of human rights lawyers for autonomy and governing themselves.

In the real world, these lawyers' associations work under the Ministry of Justice and impose discipline, as Representative Pitts has already recognized, on lawyers. Normally they operate quietly. They try to have chats, informal talks, with lawyers to discourage them from taking part in a broad range of cases. If they do not discourage them from taking part, they certainly require them to report, to accept guidance, in the handling of sensitive cases. These cases include highly controversial, sensitive political cases, like those involving Xinjiang and Uyghur independence claims, or Tibet, or people who want to organize democratic parties.

Falun Gong has been one of the most controversial categories. The systematic abuses received by the Falun Gong worshipers have been a highly sensitive point, and most lawyers are not permitted to represent Falun Gong defendants, and those who do are highly controlled.

"House church" people have also often found legal advice is not available to them, or is inadequate. There have been many cases involving claims against government for rather mundane activities. Corruption questions involving local officials, attempts to subject women to arbitrary birth control procedures, forced eviction of people from their housing and relocating them to places they don't want to be. Even civil cases encounter interference with lawyers on occasion.

Professor Feinerman's statement, which I looked at briefly before the hearing, has many good examples of land transactions, environmental disputes, collective labor disputes, compensation for tainted milk products, earthquake victims; all of these cases have been cases where many lawyers—public interest lawyers, human rights lawyers—have wanted to take part and have often been refused or restrained in their effort to take part. The most recent case involves the Charter 08 organizer, Liu Xiaobo, who was not permitted to retain the famous human rights lawyer, Mo Shaoping.

Now, lawyers who don't follow the informal advice/suggestions/instructions of the local lawyers' association or the judicial bureau of their city suffer many sanctions. Their license to practice law may be suspended, it can be revoked.

A most recent technique used is to get the local lawyers' association, as Representative Pitts recognized, not to approve the renewal of lawyers' licenses and that effectively denies these people the ability to practice law. And as has been indicated, their law firms are coerced to restrain them, stop them, or fire them, move them out; there are a variety of techniques we do not have time to consider.

Moreover—and this is rarely focused on—there are Communist Party organizations in these law firms. These law firms have Party organizations, like every social unit in China. They have been strengthened so that most law firms now will have a Party organization, a Party branch, that may reinforce discipline.

Now, for the lawyers most unresponsive to the guidance of the authorities, criminal process has been invoked. A number of people have been sent to prison on a variety of pretexts. Criminal law in every country tends to be rather broad, and in China it is especially vague. That is how lawyers who have already lost their license, like Gao Zhisheng in Beijing and Zheng Enchong in Shanghai, have been sentenced to prison.

In Shenzhen, a lawyer, Liu Yao, was sentenced to prison, and only the petition of over 500 local lawyers got him out after 16 months. But in all such cases, these people who are convicted of crime lose their right to practice law forever, and that certainly makes a major inroad on their ability to earn a living and their capacity to carry out public interest work.

Moreover, even self-taught, "barefoot" lawyers, who aren't really licensed lawyers but who, through self-study and experience and practice, have managed to learn something about law and who play an important role in some places in the countryside, have been sent to prison.

Chen Guangcheng is the most famous example. He's still got about a year to serve. I know all these people. I know Gao, I know Zheng, I know Liu Yao, I know Chen Guangcheng. These are marvelous people. They don't deserve criminal punishment.

Another case involves Guo Feixiong, I didn't have space for it in my introduction, but should mention it. He's another "barefoot" lawyer, convicted for operating a business without a license because he published a book about eight years ago without having the requisite approval. He got five years for that, an unusually heavy sentence.

The worst aspect of this from my point of view is the physical intimidation that many "rights" lawyers are informally exposed to. Today is the 156th day since Gao Zhisheng was "disappeared," to use the English version of Latin American parlance. You remember the techniques of Latin American dictatorships? Well, is China starting that?

Gao had been convicted. He'd been released on a suspended sentence, but he didn't comply with all the demands made on him, especially not to reveal torture he had already suffered, and he has not been heard from since his abduction. Absurdly, the Chinese Embassy in Washington, in response to congressional inquiry, has said he's on probation and he's free. Well, if he's free, no one knows where he is. Many people fear he's dead. So, this is not a happy situation.

Of course, many lawyers have been beaten. Professor Feinerman gives some details on that. I know some myself. I've seen the bruises just a few weeks ago in Beijing on some of the lawyers who were more recently attacked. And, of course, I know Professor Teng Biao, who was kidnapped, a hood put over his face, taken to a remote place, held for hours, and threatened. This is Hitlerian, thuggish behavior. It's not appropriate, given China's accomplishments, China's great progress in economic and social matters and the desire of the Chinese leadership to have their country recognized as having a civilized government. It should stop.

And, of course, in their daily lives, many "rights" lawyers are monitored. If I call a rights lawyer up and say, "Can you come for dinner tomorrow?" He says, "I have to ask my keeper who's outside." He calls back and says, "No, they won't permit me to come. If I want to go to the office tomorrow I can't go to dinner with you tonight, but maybe I can send a substitute." It's their daily life.

The worst case of this type I know is Zheng Enchong's. He already served three years in prison. He also finished one year of restriction on his political rights. Nevertheless, he is daily living a nightmare in terms of being restricted, being beaten, having his family discriminated against. His daughter had to flee to America because the authorities made it plain she had no future in China.

Zheng Enchong does not deserve this. He is a splendid person. I tried to visit him in 2006. Six policemen stopped me from going into his apartment. I kept saying to them, "What's your authority for doing this? There's no legal basis for this that I know of." They simply said, "We're police." I asked again and they said, "We're police." I said, "Look, in Shanghai you're always saying that you're better than the rest of the country with respect to the rule of law. 'We're police' isn't a good enough answer."

So it makes me think, if Victor Li were to have a sequel to his stimulating 1977 book, called "Law Without Lawyers," maybe we should call it "Lawlessness Without Lawyers." If you don't have human rights lawyers, what you get is lawlessness.

There are only a few minutes left. I just want to comment briefly on three other important aspects. One is human rights lawyers and political reform. There is an understandable debate going on in China among the human rights law community: should human rights lawyers take part in active political reform? Should they call for an end to the monopoly of power of the Chinese Communist Party? Or should they simply try to make the best of their bad professional situation, fighting for the public interest and human rights with one arm tied behind their back because of all the restraints they suffer?

Most of the lawyers take the latter position. Gao Zhisheng did not. I talked with him about this and I said I admired his view that without political reform of a significant nature there never would be a genuine rule of law in China. But I also said, "If you take this position in public, you're not going to be available to help people any more. You're not going to be on the street." Within four months, he wasn't, and he has suffered terribly.

Some other "rights" lawyers take the view that they are professionals, not political figures. Yet they're not merely like dentists, they recognize the need for law reform. They take part in legislative reform. They handle individual cases the best they can. Most of them remain on the street, and even though they're punished in the ways I've indicated, this valiant group continues.

Mo Shaoping has been the embodiment of the professional lawyer who publicly keeps his nose out of politics. Yet even he was so frustrated last year that he signed the famous Charter 08, which surprised people. But I think he will continue to be in the professional mode, not looking for active political reform and leaving that to others.

There are a lot of restrictions on lawyers' daily practice. Of course, this Commission has considered them before, and many people have written about them, including myself, and my statement refers to them. I won't linger on that.

I will just say that the active human rights lawyers, not only in criminal prosecutions, are limited in what they're allowed to do and are subject to a considerable number of unfair restrictions. Many basic questions have yet to be dealt with, for example: should witnesses come to court in a major criminal case so they can be cross-examined or should the statement they gave the police be sufficient evidence and essentially unchallenged?

There are also problems with supposedly "non-criminal" sanctions. The infamous *laodong jiaoyang,* "reeducation through labor," for example. Lawyers have generally not been allowed to play a role in the process of determining whether somebody should be sent off for as many as three years of what amounts to criminal punishment under a different name.

There is pressure now to try to improve the procedures because the Ministry of Public Security is desperately trying to retain "reeducation through labor," which gives the police alone the power to put you away for as long as three years; no lawyer, no prosecutor, no judge is necessary.

In reviewing such police determinations, there is a modest role for courts and lawyers but it is modest. Constitutional questions also are not open to lawyers at this point. The courts cannot consider them, the National People's Congress Standing Committee, which can, is not really functioning in this respect, so lawyers are also frustrated there. If China adheres to the International Covenant on Civil and Political Rights, the role of lawyers will be expanded, at least in principle, and we hope in practice.

Just a final point about "barefoot" lawyers. The Chinese countryside is sadly lacking in legal services. Some counties—a few years ago, 206 counties—had no lawyers whatever. People need legal advice. "Barefoot" lawyers are one response to this, people who do not have formal legal education and are not qualified lawyers, but who, nevertheless, can play a role when regular lawyers fail to do the job. Unfortunately, some members of the legal profession oppose "barefoot" lawyers. They think they'll only make the reputation of lawyers worse regarding corruption and incompetence.

I think that is short-sighted. I think we should follow the example of the former dean of Tsinghua Law School, Wang Chenguang, in training "barefoot" lawyers to play a role in the rural areas, otherwise people in the countryside will often have no way to challenge arbitrary rule, whether it's a question of arbitrary taxation, land deprivation, or whatever.

There are many questions that ought to be considered here, and I am grateful to the Commission for giving us the opportunity to discuss them. Thank you very much.

[The prepared statement of Mr. Cohen appears in the appendix.]

Ms. OLDHAM-MOORE. Thank you, Mr. Cohen. Commissioner Pitts had to go vote. He'll be back.

Nury Turkel has an obligation that he cannot avoid. He'll give brief remarks, and then he unfortunately has to depart.

Please, Nury.

STATEMENT OF NURY TURKEL, ATTORNEY WITH KIRSTEIN & YOUNG, PLLC

Mr. TURKEL. Thank you very much for organizing this panel discussion.

I'm going to use one minute of my time to clarify a couple of things about what is happening in Urumqi. First of all, we oppose any type of violence for any reason. I'd like to make it absolutely clear that the Chinese Government's accusation of Uyghur organizations instigating the incidents in Urumqi is false.

The other point I'd like to clarify is the number of casualties. The government says 156 deaths. They haven't broken down the ethnic numbers. From what we heard through a Radio Free Asia interview with a Uyghur individual from Urumqi, several hundred Uyghurs have been shot in front of Xinjiang University, Xinjiang Medical University, and in Central Square.

I wanted to clarify another point. The Guangdong incident sparked the incidents but that's not the only reason as to why the Uyghurs took to the streets to demonstrate. In the last six decades, particularly since 9/11, the Uyghurs lose out on every front; polit-ical, economic, and social.

Considering the Chinese history of heavy-handed and brutal crackdowns on political dissenters, the Uyghurs took to the streets carrying the Chinese flags last Sunday. They did not intend to turn the demonstration into a violent incident. It turned into violence after the Chinese started firing tear gas and shooting at the dem-onstrators. The demonstration was mostly organized by students. A week ago, the Turkish President delivered a very interesting speech at Xinjiang University and most of the students who partici-pated in the demonstration were from Xinjiang University.

Today, we're discussing the lack of access to lawyers and Chinese Government harassment of rights lawyers in China. I'd like to point out that there will be a mass arrest, torture, and execution in the coming weeks and months. Those detained and accused will not have access to fair judicial process or lawyers.

Speaking of which, the Uyghur political prisoners or demonstra-tors participating in the 1997 uprising in Ghulja are still lan-guishing in prison. I don't believe that any of them have had access to fair judicial process. I had a chance to interview two of the former political prisoners who participated in the 1997 demonstra-tion. One of them happened to be a former Guantanamo inmate who now lives in Albania. He said he didn't have any access to law-yers. He was subject to torture and long imprisonment.

For Uyghurs, representing or being represented is extremely dif-ficult, because anything Uyghurs have done could be easily trans-lated into a political crime that is separatism or terrorism. So any Chinese or Uyghur lawyers cannot even get close to representing, or even talking to, the Uyghur prisoners in Chinese prisons. It's simply too risky to represent Uyghur cases.

Recently, there has been one other legal need that has emerged for Uyghurs: losing their properties, particularly in Kashgar. As you may have read recently, the Chinese Government is demol-ishing the Old City of Kashgar, and that has resulted in many Uyghurs losing their real properties. And they're not being fairly compensated.

When they ask for their lawyers' help, their response is that "it's a government policy and if I represent you, I'll be in trouble. I can-not get involved, even though this is a property interests and com-pensation-related issue. If I represent you and go to the courts with you, then the government will take away my license. Sorry, I can-not help you." That has been a typical response from lawyers.

Recently I've conducted interviews and found out that there are no Uyghur rights lawyers. Basically, there is no Uyghur Gao Zhisheng. There are some Uyghurs who represent cases involving petty crimes. As long as it does not involve criticizing government or criticizing government officials, the Uyghur lawyers take cases involving petty crimes.

I'd like to use a few examples to highlight the situation, particu-larly the political prisoner situation in Xinjiang. The most famous case is the case of Rebiya Kadeer's children. They were initially taken into custody for tax evasion. When that happened, Rebiya Kadeer's family tried to get a lawyer. And most of them flatly re-jected it because of her name, because of her family history.

They initially thought that it might be all right to represent them since it was tax-related issues. Then later, the government charged Ms. Kadeer's sons for crimes of separatism and endangering state security. They made the lawyers keep their hands off the cases. So one of her children was sentenced to seven years in prison and the other one was sentenced to nine years in prison.

One other famous case involves a Canadian citizen—his name is Hussein Celil—who traveled to Uzbekistan with a Canadian passport. At the request of the Chinese Government, he was deported to China. To this day, Canadian officials, Canadian lawyers cannot get access to him. It's been more than three years since his arrest. A couple of years ago, he was sentenced to life in prison.

I talked to his lawyer last week. His name is Chris McLeod. He said he even tried to hire a local lawyer, with the help of a group of Falun Gong practitioners who have access to a local rights lawyer. They invited the Chinese lawyer from Beijing. But that courageous lawyer was harassed and even received death threats. His family was upset that he's representing a separatist and terrorist. Then the lawyer backed off.

So I wish I could tell you good stories. But there's literally nothing good coming out of the Uyghur region. Last night I was doing research to find out what is happening to this brave "barefoot" lawyer that Professor Cohen was mentioning. His name is Ilham Tohti. He is an economics professor at Beijing Nationalities University. He has been an outspoken critic of the Chinese officials in Urumqi. His point is that China has a constitution and autonomy laws. These officials, including Nur Bekri and Wang Lequan are making it difficult not only for the Uyghurs, but also the central government. They are the root cause of all the Uyghur resentment and ethnic tension.

He is the owner of a blog that the Chinese Government has accused of being used by the so-called separatists and rioters to plan Sunday's demonstration. We've found out last night that he has been taken away. We don't know his whereabouts. He said, right before his arrest on his blog, that "I always tell myself to be cool, calm, and make rational analysis. Going to the courts to resolve disputes is something that should be lawful in this society. I am my own lawyer. When my trial comes up, they'll appoint a lawyer for me. I will not trust the government to appoint a lawyer."

I'd like to end my remarks there. Thank you.

Ms. OLDHAM-MOORE. Thank you, Nury. We're very grateful that you were able to get here today. I know you had a number of other obligations. Thank you.

Professor James Feinerman, we're honored to have you. Please go ahead.

STATEMENT OF JAMES V. FEINERMAN, PROFESSOR OF ASIAN LEGAL STUDIES, GEORGETOWN UNIVERSITY LAW CENTER, CODIRECTOR, ASIAN LAW AND POLICY STUDIES PROGRAM

Mr. FEINERMAN. Thank you. I am very glad that I'm here today and that the Commission has convened this roundtable on this very important topic. I'm grateful to Representative Pitts for coming here and demonstrating with his presence the importance that is attached to this issue. I am, of course, very glad to be here with my colleagues on the panel, particularly my teacher and mentor, Mr. Cohen.

I am glad that he began by both quoting Victor Li—I'll come back to that in a second—and by saying that he was going to depart from his prepared remarks. I have some too, and I will likewise depart from them since you can read what I had to say there, and I will try to summarize them and hit a few other points along the way in the brief time that is allotted to me.

I am glad that Jerry mentioned Victor Li because I actually spoke before another hearing of this Commission about five or six years ago, and the title of my presentation then was "Lawyers Without Law," turning around the title of Victor's famous book. The point that I was making then, which I think is still valid today, is that China has lawyers. It has lots of lawyers compared to what it had when Victor wrote his book, and even for decades afterward.

But the point is that they don't really operate in a system which has the rule of law that makes the practice of what they do meaningful in the sense of promising justice to the widest range of the Chinese citizenry, although many lawyers do what lawyers do in this country and many other countries in representing clients in court and carrying out business transactions and advising people about things like taxes and family law.

But what is missing is the sense that there is an obligation on the part of lawyers and the organized bar in general to do something about the overall enjoyment of justice by the citizens of their country. I think that that's an important thing to take home from the presentations that you're roundtable today in a variety of different circumstances, whether it's the mistreatment of ethnic minorities in Xinjiang, whether it's the continuing illegal harassment—even given China's constitutional law—of religious practitioners, or some of the other cases that I'll talk about, highlighting what is in my prepared remarks.

I think it's also an important event to have this roundtable today, this month, because this month marks the 30th anniversary of China's determination to embrace the rule of law. Often the criticism that China makes or tries to deflect when it is criticized by others for lacking the rule of law is that this is a Western concept and we don't really have to explain ourselves. We're our own country, we have our own sovereignty, we have our own very long historic tradition, and we do things our way, you do things your way.

But I think as the embrace of the rule of law that began with the publication of China's first seven laws, really after the establishment of the People's Republic of China in 1979 on July 1, illustrates this is a choice the Chinese have made themselves. If they believe in their own propaganda, they have to then follow the laws that they've created for themselves.

It just isn't on to say that we can violate our own constitution because we're the final determiners of what it means. That's an objective document that other people are perfectly qualified to interpret and to call them out when it's clear hypocrisy as to what the Chinese are actually doing with regard to their own legal system.

But the fact that they decided to embrace law those three decades ago indicates that there is a need to create, and China did create, courts and lawyers to practice before them. So let me just briefly note those two things. China revived a system of courts that it actually had for a short period in the 1950s. In fact, Professor Cohen's famous book about the criminal justice system described what existed in lieu of formally organized criminal courts in that brief period of embrace of a Soviet legal model in the 1950s and early 1960s.

But when China passed these new laws in 1979, one of those laws was an organic law for the organization of People's Courts, and it made it clear that there was going to be a court system, including a full hierarchy of trial courts, appellate courts, and even a Supreme People's Court, that was going to operate in a different way than the justice system had operated previously.

But coming down to today, we can see that the court system has been consistently underfunded, starved of resources. The first judges, almost for two decades, were very poorly trained, often demobilized military officers and former police officials. You can just imagine what kind of justice a judiciary made up solely of those sorts might mete out. It's only really been in the last decade that legally trained graduates of university law faculties are beginning to assume important roles in the bench.

Just this past year, China removed a well-qualified, highly-trained former chief judge, the Supreme People's Court president, Xiao Yang, and replaced him with a totally unqualified Party hack who has no legal training, Wang Shengjun. As a result, the legal system is headed at the top by someone who lacks genuine legal qualifications and commitment to the rule of law, although we can guess from his Party background what he's probably committed to.

Also, as for lawyers, China went from a handful, fewer than a couple of hundred lawyers in 1979, many of whom had been trained even before the 1949 Communist takeover, to a system today that boasts somewhere between 130,000 and 140,000 lawyers.

But what do those lawyers do? What were they trained to do? Here, I don't mean to unjustly criticize China. In this country and many other countries as well, it's only a small handful of lawyers who go into what we call pro bono representation, representing unpopular causes, doing the Lord's work, so to speak, in areas like dealing with human rights victims, taking seriously violations of human rights, calling their own legal systems to account.

It isn't lucrative, it isn't remunerative as law practice in other areas can be. Even in countries other than China it can be fraught with dangers, some not quite so dire as they are in China, but dangers nonetheless, including possible threats to the lawyers themselves and their families.

But in China, it's been pretty clear that they have moved from a system where every lawyer was a state legal worker working in a state-run legal advisory office to a system where there are, today, private law firms. I was looking at the Web site of one of them yesterday that had offices or corresponding relationships on five continents, every bit as big and all-embracing as the largest multinational law firms based in New York or London.

It's clear that lawyers in China may be doing something very different than what we might hope, at least a reasonable representation of them would be doing with regard to protecting their citizens' rights. And here I'll just tell you two anecdotes that I think reveal what is actually been the rule with lawyers' training in China.

I remember going when I was a young associate myself in New York to an event at Columbia Law School that was organized by our colleague, Professor Randle Edwards. He had hosted the first group of Chinese who had come to be trained in law. This was 1981. The legal profession hadn't really been reestablished. None of these people had been trained as lawyers, but they were going to be expected to return and do law-related jobs in China. They spent four months at Columbia Law School getting a very thorough introduction to American law, and then they spent six months in New York City law firms learning what lawyers did, shadowing senior lawyers, and seeing a range of legal practice.

At the reception, the oldest of them, who later went on to become the head of the All China Lawyers Association, a man named Gao Zongze, handed me his card. The card had his name on it, and underneath in English it said "senior partner." I turned it over to see what it said in Chinese, and the translation was something like, "high-class lawyer." [Laughter.]

I said, "Mr. Gao, aren't you a little worried about going around representing yourself as a partner?" Chinese lawyers don't practice in law firms. Law firms aren't partnerships. There is no partnership law. He said, "Well, I learned one thing in the six months that I spent at my New York City law firm." I was eager to learn what that was. I said, "Oh really? How interesting. What was that?" He said, "The only people who get respect are senior partners."

So, if that's what it took, that's what he was going to call himself. He went on to quite a career as a practicing lawyer in China, but I think that on his agenda, and on the agenda of the organization that he headed, the human rights or civil rights of Chinese citizens was quite low, maybe even non-existent.

Likewise, I'd just mention, a few years later in 1991, actually, when I went back with the leadership of the American Bar Association to meet with our Chinese counterparts—it was a visit much-delayed for two years because of what happened in Tiananmen Square in 1989. We were meeting with people who purported to be the organizers of the first genuine private law firm in China. The firm is called Jun He, and it's gone on to some prominence in Chinese legal practice.

The incoming president of the American Bar asked one of the lawyers, a young man who had been trained at UCLA Law School and obviously had some experience in the United States before going back to China, whether or not someone like him or someone from his law firm would take on the representation of the various defendants that were accused of misdeeds in Tiananmen Square.

He very quickly saw his opening, leapt up and said, "No, no. You have to understand that given the training that we've had and all the advantages that we have and what we've learned, having us do that kind of work would be like having a brain surgeon do veterinary medicine." The room got very quiet and the incoming president became very red-faced. He was a former dean of the Florida State University Law School and a partner in a Miami law firm. He said, "I'm the incoming president of the American Bar Association and senior partner at Steel, Hector & Davis, and I do veterinary medicine." [Laughter.]

So the young man realized he had misstepped and tried to pull back, but it was pretty hard to retreat.

In the few moments that are left to me, let me just tick off the few things that I think are worth highlighting from the center of my report that you have before you. The first is to focus on the steps that the Chinese have been taking with increasingly virulent results to try to discourage lawyers from taking on these representations. It begins with harassment. It leads, in some unfortunate cases, to severe beatings, some that are permanently disfiguring and crippling to the Chinese lawyers who experience them.

It has also involved detention and jail, the illegal detention that Professor Cohen described with people such as Gao Zhisheng, but also criminal charges and jail terms, totally unjustified by all rights, and then recently this non-renewal of licenses, which basically destroys the livelihood and any future promise of these people returning to practice.

Likewise, the range of cases that I talk about in my prepared remarks is remarkably broad and it doesn't even cover the waterfront. You'll hear from other people on this panel about things that I don't mention, but people who, for example, took on representation of the Falun Gong, people who represented other disfavored groups—some of them, by the way, these representatives, these rights defenders, are not even trained lawyers.

Hu Ja, who took on the representation of HIV patients, was not a lawyer by training but has suffered the same kind of fate because he took as his cause defending the rights of these people because there are very few lawyers who are willing to take them on as clients in China.

The absolute prohibition, really, by legal means of class action lawsuits, a guiding opinion that was issued in 2006 that basically says you have to get permission if you want to represent more than 10 clients collectively, makes it impossible for large groups of aggrieved citizens to get together and seek legal representation. There are problems with those who have tried to defend people who have suffered grievous wrongs, for example, the tainted food and baby formula cases, or the Sichuan earthquake cases—the parents, family members of victims there.

The lawyers have been brought together and told in no uncertain terms that they are not to represent these people, that if they do represent these people there will be serious consequences, and that they should think not of human rights, civil liberties, or even provisions of Chinese law, but rather creating a harmonious society and making sure that there is national unity, doing nothing to damage the overall impression that the situation is excellent and constantly improving.

So at the very last, I would just mention three things that I think we should do. This goes a little bit beyond my own prepared remarks' conclusion. First, is I think that the American Bar Association and other bar associations, state and local, and bar associations in foreign countries as well, should voice their concerns about this, develop resolutions, and make it clear that we have our counterparts in China and we're concerned about them. I don't think that this has been done enough to bring home the seriousness. China would respect, for example, the prominence of American lawyers who occupy a somewhat different and more protected position in their society than lawyers do in China.

I think, second, the United States and other foreign governments should make it clear through their foreign ministries, through their ministries of justice, and also through their congresses and parliaments, as Representative Pitts has done here, that this is a matter of great concern to political leaders and this is something that we will take seriously in our future dealings with China if they don't make some progress on this front.

Finally, I think that, as with fora like this here at the Commission, that in every other place where we can possibly get a hearing it's important to keep up the publicity and the outreach to people who are in these dire circumstances in China. I know Professor Cohen, for example, and a number of my counterparts, law professors in the United States, have done our best to try and make sure that we remain in contact in whatever way we legally can with our Chinese colleagues, especially those in the practicing bar who have experienced these very severe repressions.

But it's hard, and it requires persistence. It will be helpful to have a lot of other people doing this work as well rather than relying on just a small group of interested people who have been trying to carry out this enterprise under very adverse circumstances for, unfortunately, a very long period of time.

Thank you.

[The prepared statement of Mr. Feinerman appears in the appendix.]

Ms. OLDHAM-MOORE. Thank you, Mr. Feinerman.

Before turning to Bob Fu, at 11:10 we'll open the floor to questions from the audience.

Bob, please begin. Thank you.

STATEMENT OF BOB (XIQIU) FU, FOUNDER AND PRESIDENT, CHINAAID ASSOCIATION (CAA)

Mr. FU. Thank you. Thank you for the invitation to this panel with Professor Cohen, Professor Feinerman, and Mr. Turkel. I very much appreciate the hard work and concern of the CECC Commissioners, including Congressman Pitts and many others, and, of course, the CECC senior staffers.

I have been involved with the training of human rights lawyers, especially in the areas of international law, since 2004. We actually invited the first delegation, in 2005, to the United States. We had some training with the NYU Law School. Professor Cohen has been involved.

Recently I have been receiving many messages from lawyers in China about their license cancellations or their licenses have not been renewed by the Beijing Lawyers Association. This is not only unnecessary and unjust, but also an unprecedented development. As far as I know, that we can confirm, so far, 19 lawyers were already imprisoned and this year the 19 lawyers at this time are unable to practice their law. They are: Jiang Tianyong, Li Heping, Li Xiongbing, Li Fuchun, Wang Yajun, Guo Shaofei, Cheng Hai, Tang Jitian, Yang Huiwen, Tong Chaoping, Liu Guitao, Xie Yanyi, Wen

Haibo, Liu Wei, Zhang Lihui, Zhang Chengmao, Zhang Xingshui, Wei Liangyue, and Sun Wenbing.

These attorneys have always persisted in providing legal assistance for clients to safeguard their legitimate rights. The report I have seen, in an open letter to the Ministry of Justice on July 2, most clearly explains the situation with the license denials and points out the root problems and effects of this on the national level.

This letter was written by 31 Chinese intellectuals, 23 in Beijing, 7 in other areas in China, and 1 Australian. I request that the full text of this open letter be entered into the record.

Ms. OLDHAM-MOORE. Yes.

Mr. FU. Thank you.

I will read a few key points of this letter. It says,

> We think this case is entirely a violation of the law. As a social organization in the legal industry, the Beijing Lawyers Association has no right to restrict or deprive its members of their right to practice. In the past, there were cases in which the Beijing Lawyers Association deprived some human rights lawyers of their qualifications to practice, but that was considered an illegal overstepping of its authority. Now it has forced many law firms to stop the practice and made several hundred lawyers unable to practice, which is all the more astonishing. Such illegal, absurd, and perverse acts that violate common sense will bring serious, bad consequences to society.
>
> On July 18, 2008, the Ministry of Justice promulgated management methods in attorneys' practice and management methods on law firms which officially annulled the annual registration system of the attorneys. This time, the Beijing Lawyers Association issued a notice and changed "registration" to "register" and totally disregarded the principles of the Ministry of Justice in that the specific methods for annual evaluation shall be provided by a Ministry of Justice.
>
> First of all, it will further worsen the environment for rule of law in society by taking advantage of the authorization from Beijing's Bureau of Justice and the Beijing Lawyers Association suppresses and takes revenge on human rights lawyers as it wishes. Most of these attorneys are top-notch, outstanding attorneys who have the highest awareness of the rule of law among 10,000 attorneys in Beijing.
>
> Second, cancellation of licenses of a large number of attorneys has undermined to a great extent the strategic elements for building a harmonious society.
>
> Third, canceling the right to practice of so many rights defense attorneys is a provocation on the social conscience.

The first part of my recommendation for the congressional response is to base the response on this recommendation from this open letter to the Ministry of Justice. It is a very clear, straightforward framework on which I think U.S. congressional response to Beijing can be based.

I will read part of this recommendation letter, the recommendation from the open letter. It says,

It is our belief that as the highest traditional administrative organ of our country, the Ministry of Justice should not ignore such a violation of law by the Beijing Municipal Bureau of Justice and the Beijing Lawyers Association, worsening the environment for rule of law, undermining the social harmony, and challenging the social conscience. We hope the Ministry of Justice can, in the principle of upholding the spirit of the rule of law as proposed at the 17th People's Congress, order the Beijing Municipal Bureau of Justice and Beijing Lawyers Association to withdraw their decision, correct their mistakes, and restore the rights lawyers' right to practice, and apologize to the people in various circles of life so as to solve this problem in a fair, reasonable, and legal way.

I appreciate the clear statements in this letter which really explains not only their concern, but also the national effects of these licensed denials. The effects which ultimately concern—especially because unfortunately they show an utter disregard for the rule of law by the largest country in the world.

One question to be addressed by this panel is, what is the relationship between these lawyers, the Chinese Government, and the Chinese Communist Party? This brings up an intriguing point because these human rights lawyers have been moving forward according to the proposal from the 17th People's Congress to promote the spirit of the rule of law and the realization of the rule of law in various jobs of state.

A simple list has been compiled of each lawyer whose license has been revoked or not renewed and the important incidents and the cases the lawyers have been involved with, and the categories mentioned in this list, including the poisonous milk incident, the abnormal deaths while the victim was in custody, representing house churches and Falun Gong practitioners, and reeducation through labor cases, the rights of migrant workers and ethnic minorities, and rights of HIV patients, and the cases of underground brick kilns in Shanxi Province.

Which of these cases should the government shrink from having represented by a professional lawyer? Does not rule of law necessitate the vulnerability to transparency? Transparency and the rule of law, in some of these cases, might necessitate acknowledgement of unjust measures or inappropriate use of authority. That is unfortunately a consistent possibility in any government because of human nature. What is not a necessity or acceptable is repression of lawyers who are implementing the rule of law.

So, I will mention briefly about Gao Zhisheng's case. Professor Cohen already mentioned it, but we have launched a campaign called FreeGao.com, a campaign since March. So far, we have received over 102,000 signatures up until today, from Bosnia to Saudi Arabia, from Turkey to Zimbabwe. People from all over the world signed to urge the Chinese Government to tell us where Gao is and what his condition is about.

So of course, these developments strengthen the play of the U.S. Congress, to publicly affirm the truth and justice, investigate these issues. I understand, after meeting with the chairman, Congressman Jim McGovern, who is the chairman of the Tom Lantos Commission, he will write a joint letter, along with a Member of Congress, today or tomorrow to send to the Chinese Ambassador to ask the whereabouts of Mr. Gao.

Finally, I want to urge the Obama Administration officials and the senior U.S. diplomats at the Embassy in Beijing to publicly, regularly, and frequently meet with these freedom fighters in and outside China when they are available.

Ms. OLDHAM-MOORE. Thank you.

Mr. FU. Thank you.

[The prepared statement of Mr. Fu, the Open Letter, and the Final Compiled Translated Lawyers' Statements appear in the appendix.]

Ms. OLDHAM-MOORE. The ChinaAid Association has done a tremendous job raising the profile of the Gao case on the Hill. Thank you.

We're delighted to have Congressman Wu with us. It's nice to see you, sir. He's just rejoined the Commission this year. So, we're delighted to see you here today.

Now at this stage in the proceedings we open it up to the audience for questions.

Congressman Wu, would you like to say something?

Representative WU. No. I think I will——

Ms. OLDHAM-MOORE. I think we hijacked you.

Representative WU. I will listen very happily to the Q&A for as long as I can before my next obligation.

Ms. OLDHAM-MOORE. Terrific. Thank you so much. The first question from the audience. Do we have anybody? Yes, sir; in the front.

AUDIENCE PARTICIPANT. Thank you. Mr. Feinerman, you've commented that you felt it was necessary that American lawyers, bar associations, and so forth get involved in this process to try to help the situation, rights defenders. I've been trying to work on that for about a year now with Dr. Fu and we're not having a lot of success. Do you have any suggestions on how we get these bar associations to come on board and understand that lawyers across the world are our brothers and sisters and that we need to let them know that we will stick with them?

Mr. FEINERMAN. Well, I have two practical suggestions based on my own experience doing this. Twenty years ago in the aftermath of Tiananmen, we did get the American Bar Association, as well as the New York City Bar, to make statements that were formal resolutions adopted by the Bar Association and such about what happened in the aftermath then. I think that the time has come to try and refire those sorts of connections.

Bar associations in general usually have two ways of doing this. One is to contact the top bar leadership, the executive director or whoever is in charge of the bar association, and try and get a resolution on the table, usually at their annual meetings, but sometimes they can do it outside of that forum as well.

Then second, they almost all have at least one committee, and sometimes multiple committees, that are involved with questions of human rights, contact with foreign bars. The American Bar Association, for example, has as one of its enumerated goals Goal VIII, which is fostering the rule of law around the world. So, there is a

Goal VIII group inside the American Bar Association, but there is also a separate committee on individual rights and responsibilities.

The Section on International Law has a China law group, although because of their interest in pursuing practice and contacts with China and clients both in the United States and China who want to stay on the right side of the government, they may not be your first point of contact or your best ally with regard to this.

But I agree, there are like-minded people in these organizations, even in the China law subcommittees, who would say that this has reached such a stage and the conduct is so outrageous, that we believe a general statement that talks about the kinds of concerns that lawyers abroad have for their counterparts in China is certainly well within the limits that even a restrictive government might place on those kind of undertakings.

Ms. OLDHAM-MOORE. Thank you.

Yes, sir? Congressman Wu, then Jerry Cohen, I know, wants to say something.

Representative WU. If I may just add a point to that response. I'll just speak up a little bit. When we were dealing with the Pakistani situation where lawyers were taking such a leading role, I found that law schools were especially valuable venues and many of the deans were quite amenable to contacting their faculty. One might find a little bit more hesitation in those law schools that have extensive programs in China, but I think that the academic community is a good source of help in addition to the bar organizations.

Thank you.

Ms. OLDHAM-MOORE. Thank you.

Professor Cohen?

Mr. COHEN. I think those ideas we just heard from both speakers are excellent. Committees have formed in various places to try to be helpful. Hong Kong has taken the lead with its human rights lawyers group to support Chinese human rights lawyers. The Taipei Bar Association and the Taiwan Bar Association have been supportive. The International Bar Association has just issued a good statement about the problems of Chinese lawyers. In New York, our city bar association has an active human rights committee and a committee on Asian law that are concerned.

A group of us in New York last year formed a Committee to Support Chinese Lawyers that is centered at Fordham University Law School's Leitner Center. It does just what the Congressman has said should be done. The American Bar Association [ABA], of course, does very good work in Chinese law reform, including human rights, criminal justice, lawyers' problems, and that is to be commended. NYU Law School cooperates closely with the ABA in this respect.

I think our deans and our university presidents have to seize more occasions. For example, this year there will be a number of anniversaries of Chinese law schools being established 30, in some cases, 100 years ago. American deans are invited. I think, instead of passing up those occasions, they should participate and make very strong statements about the importance of protecting human rights lawyers and the importance of protecting law faculty people who not only teach, write, and publish to the extent they're allowed to, but often take part in active cases and therefore suffer sanctions. So I think this is a very good question to have raised.

Ms. OLDHAM-MOORE. Thank you.

Next questioner. Jim Geheran is up next.

Mr. GEHERAN. Hi. Jim Geheran—questions to Professor Cohen—lawyers do not—characterize—the situation in China. One of the issues that I see before us as—China is that our foreign policy tends to compartmentalize the issue of human rights and we fail to see—to make human rights the centerpiece of our foreign policy in regard to—this morning—essentially exists in terms of, without the rule of law—make a conforming argument to support the statement that—that the world community should not rely on countries who do not rely on their own citizens.

Ms. OLDHAM-MOORE. Okay.

Mr. GEHERAN [continuing].—That statement really supports——

Ms. OLDHAM-MOORE. Thank you.

Professor Cohen?

Mr. COHEN. Well, we have witnessed the struggle of every new Federal administration in this country to adopt an appropriate human rights policy, one that will be good across the board, that is not selectively applied. One complaint China has sometimes justifiably made is that we're very selective in our targets for human rights. We neglect many of our friends, so-called, for their human rights violations but we focus only on certain other countries. So, consistency is important.

Second, our own behavior is crucial. I think one of the most profound things anybody has ever said was the Scottish poet Robert Burns, who said, "Oh wad the Lord, this giftie gie us to see oursels as ithers see us." Our own conduct, especially recently in the Bush Administration, the second Bush Administration, has made us very vulnerable to charges of hypocrisy when we start to point out the human rights weaknesses in other countries.

I think one good thing China has done is to issue an annual human rights report on U.S. Government behavior. As long as it's factual, I think it's very helpful. If it's merely propagandistic, one-sided, et cetera, then it isn't. But we all benefit from criticism of that nature. Our own conduct is very important.

Now, we've watched Secretary Clinton try to come to grips with the question, where does human rights in China fit into our broader China needs, because we need Chinese cooperation just as China needs our cooperation? I'm hoping to see a more vigorous, case-oriented discussion between the United States and China and one that will include not only government officials from both countries, but also non-officials who are more specialized, who have more knowledge than officials.

This Commission could recommend an idea that was floating around the State Department at the end of the second Bush Administration, which would be to initiate a real human rights dialogue, one that discusses concrete cases. Chinese officials love to talk in the abstract. They don't like to deal with concrete cases. In the extreme case of Gao Zhisheng, we see they're not prepared to tell the truth even if they choose to respond on concrete cases, but I think this would be important for the Commission to encourage that kind of dialogue.

Ms. OLDHAM-MOORE. Thank you.

Kara Abramson, please.

Ms. ABRAMSON. Thank you. Kara Abramson with the Congressional-Executive Commission on China. I will direct this question to Mr. Cohen.

I understand the sensitivities of working on an issue like Xinjiang, which you raised in your testimony, but many issues are sensitive. Falun Gong is sensitive, and yet lawyers take on cases defending Falun Gong. So my question is, as rights defense lawyers pursue sensitive cases despite the risks, why are they not actively pursuing cases involving Xinjiang. I recognize that cases involving issues like separatism are extremely sensitive, but I wonder if there might be areas where there is room to push the envelope, such as cases involving employment discrimination based on ethnicity. I am interested in hearing your thoughts on that, please. Thank you.

Mr. COHEN. There are lots of needs in China for lawyers that are not yet being filled. You're pointing out some of them. Labor law is an opportunity. There are a number of firms operating not only from the management side, but from the migrant labor, the human rights, side. But there is much more that can be done.

Environment. Think of all the environmental challenges China confronts and the role that litigation might assume. Litigation that is happening is interesting, important, but merely a drop in the bucket. Every issue you turn to needs much more Chinese legal talent. The problem is how to create the conditions that make it attractive, not merely permissible, for lawyers to take part in these matters.

Professor Feinerman has alluded to the fact that most lawyers in China are not big moneymakers. There are some firms that do very well. They charge international-type fees, but they're a minority. Most lawyers are struggling to make a living. We have to figure out ways of making human rights practice possible, like compensating lawyers for successful environmental litigation or successful labor litigation. These ideas are gradually developing.

So there's a law practice area between a commercial practice with no political implications and a human rights practice that deals with things that are highly sensitive, like Falun Gong or democracy. There's quite a broad area of important cases, including open government information, where the Chinese Government is not necessarily going to be oppressive and where it increasingly will see the benefits of having law and lawyers.

Ms. ABRAMSON. Thank you. Do you think that as this space you've discussed opens up, there will be more of an interest in pursuing cases in Xinjiang, particularly in less sensitive areas like employment discrimination?

Mr. COHEN. As has been pointed out, the attempt to use lawyers in Xinjiang, Tibet, Mongolia, these highly sensitive so-called "separatist" areas, has proved to be very difficult. The Communist Party is led by people who do not have much understanding of the rule of law. Even Li Keqiang, a member of the Politburo Standing Committee who is a graduate of Peking University Law School in the class of 1982, has not taken a law reform role.

The people who run the legal system are police and Party activists who reflect their experience. The head of the Chinese Communist Party Central Political Legal Committee is the former Minister of Public Security. He doesn't know much about law, but he knows what he likes. What he likes is "harmony." They are quick always to use repression as the way to give the appearance of harmony.

The new head of the courts is not a legal specialist but a party person who is there to reinforce party controls on the courts. The new head of the Ministry of Justice is a Party Apparatchik, a nice woman who really hasn't got much interest in the kinds of problems we're discussing today or much sensitivity about them. This is too bad.

So the prospect immediately after the 17th Party Congress has not been good for promoting the kinds of things we eventually hope the Party leadership will come to see. There will someday be leaders in the Standing Committee of the Politburo of the Party who will see the importance of better legal institutions to stability, to harmony. We've been through this in South Korea under General Park. We've been through this in Taiwan under Chiang Kai-Shek. Dictators always talk about stability and therefore the need for repression, but eventually modernization comes, education, many other factors, and we see their successors take a more enlightened view. In the Communist system you never know what the highest leaders will do until they become the highest leaders.

Nobody knew what Khruschev would do before he introduced de-Stalinization in 1956. Nobody knew what Gorbachev, who was trained in law, would do based on his previous record until he got to the top. Someday there will be leaders in China's Politburo who will try to do for law what Zhu Rongji did for economics and economic reform. We have to rely on that. There's enormous support for law reform and better legal institutions in the Chinese people now, especially the poorer people, the disenfranchised people, not the elite. Bourgeois law in the West has always resulted from the rising bourgeoisie. In China, the rising bourgeoisie, the entrepreneurs, resort to other methods. They are benefiting from the system. They don't want to use law, they use connections, they use money, et cetera.

I remember asking the businessman-husband of a Chinese judge I knew: "Do you ever use lawyers?" He said, "No." I said, "Why not?" He said, "I don't need them for contracts." I said, "What about disputes? Don't you have disputes?" He said, "I have a lot of disputes. But why would I use lawyers for disputes? My wife is a judge." [Laughter].

Ms. OLDHAM-MOORE. Thank you.

Jim Feinerman, please.

Mr. FEINERMAN. This is just a footnote on the question about lawyers in Xinjiang. I think there is a problem here both with ethnicity and language that needs to be recognized. The problem is a tri-fold one. On the first point, there are probably very few lawyers trained in Xinjiang, Tibet, or other ethnic minority regions in China who represent their own people, so having to rely on Han lawyers creates a problem. Second, the capacity of these areas in terms of courts and the ability to allow people to access the legal system, even having a well-staffed bar in those localities, is very poor compared to the rest of China, and that may be purposely so to limit the kinds of claims that people in those areas might make.

Then finally, I think it is going to wait until people rise up from these groups to assume their place. In the United States, we had the great civil rights revolution that we had largely because we had black lawyers who were pursuing a cause that they were personally very invested in.

With Thurgood Marshall arguing, you get a kind of representation that I think—even though very capable white lawyers were working behind the scenes and up front with the National Association for the Advancement of Colored People [NAACP]—other groups just couldn't do. I think that that is what has to happen in China for those groups, those ethnic communities to sort of feel that they have genuine access to the legal system.

Ms. OLDHAM-MOORE. Thank you. We're going to go for 10 more minutes.

AUDIENCE PARTICIPANT. Good morning. Thank you for allowing me. My son has been——

Ms. OLDHAM-MOORE. This is a question?

AUDIENCE PARTICIPANT. Yes.

Ms. OLDHAM-MOORE. Thank you.

AUDIENCE PARTICIPANT. My son has been imprisoned in China since March. We were just informed by the U.S. Consulate, so this is a very personal nature and I prefer not to introduce myself in a public forum.

So the question is, is there a lawyer somewhere that can help our son be repatriated to come back home to the United States? We have the U.S. Consulate able to visit him once a month so far, but the letters that he has written us have been blocked from our eyes. Several Chinese lawyers have written to him, asking to represent him, but the prison authorities have blocked him from receiving those letters. So, there is only so much the U.S. Consulate can do. How do we proceed in the face of what this panel can share? Perhaps Professor Cohen, Professor Feinerman, or anyone would have a suggestion.

Ms. OLDHAM-MOORE. It's a complex question, and I've talked to your husband about this. Her son is in jail in China. She's having difficulty getting access to counsel. Her son has had consular access, with a good consulate officer. What should she do next?

Mr. COHEN. Well, if you need help finding a good Chinese criminal lawyer, certainly some of us can make suggestions. That's the first thing one does. You're already getting the active help of the American Citizen Services Unit within the Embassy, I take it, or the local consulate. But the first thing is to try to secure Chinese legal advisors and then work with them.

AUDIENCE PARTICIPANT. It's really hard to know how to pick a Chinese lawyer, given all the things you've discussed about the limited role that they play and the limited freedom they have to practice their law. How do we, from here, pick one?

Mr. COHEN. There are people who have lots of experience in this field, unfortunately.

AUDIENCE PARTICIPANT. That's wonderful. Thank you.

Ms. OLDHAM-MOORE. Yes. Thank you.

Mr. FEINERMAN. Can I just add one thing about this?

Ms. OLDHAM-MOORE. Yes.

Mr. FEINERMAN. This is not an uncommon experience, unfortunately. Professor Cohen and I were just quoted yesterday in an article in the Wall Street Journal involving business people who have been detained basically because contract negotiations didn't turn out in a way that was favorable to the Chinese party, and the solution was to imprison a Chinese who had foreign nationality, but was originally born in mainland China, and three Chinese employees, and basically say you're going to get out when we get the deal that we want.

This is a big, multinational company that has access to high-class legal representation, has probably already retained lawyers both inside and outside of China to deal with this. So I wish I could offer you more consolation in that this thing will be resolved very quickly, but as you already know from your experience to date, this is something that can drag on for quite a while.

It seems that justice will not be forthcoming, although sometimes the one word of positive advice I can provide is that if there's a pretext that allows a kind of face-saving way out for the Chinese, such as a medical condition that justifies parole or something like that, that often—so if your son has anything from diabetes to serious acne, I would say, start working that for all that it's worth, because that may be a way to say, we call on your mercy for medical leave. It's sort of a subterfuge and it doesn't address the underlying injustice of the system, but your main goal now probably is getting your son out and home.

AUDIENCE PARTICIPANT. Right. Thank you so much.

Ms. OLDHAM-MOORE. Thank you. Thank you.

Professor Cohen, some last remarks, then we'll close down.

Mr. COHEN. Yes. The first thing, and what you say makes me recognize the importance of stating it, is what kind of a case is it? If it's like this Australian case in which Rio Tinto executives are involved, the first question is, is it a "state secrets" case? If the State Security Agency or the Public Security Agency decides to call it a "state secrets" case, then the lawyer has no access unless the police agree to it, and usually the police don't until their investigation is over. It may take many months. At the point that their investigation is over and they recommend prosecution, often a lawyer can't do too much, and certainly is very limited.

One of the troubling aspects of the Chinese system is that there is no effective means for challenging the "state secrets" claim of the investigators or the certification by the National State Secrets Bureau that any documents or information involved are indeed state secrets. That is why I hope that, in the revision of the state secrets law that is about to occur 20 years after the first one came into being, there will be some improvement, but it's not clear that that will be the case.

Second, we need to consider the question of fairness, of how universal are standards of what we call "due process." China now is awash in nationalism. There is a new Chinese pride, a new feeling of, "we don't need these foreigners to tell us what to do, we'll do it our way." In principle, this may sound attractive, but in practice, in detail, what does it mean for fairness, for due process for a legal system? Will it meet at least the minimum standards of the world community? What do China's leaders and people want in this respect?

I was just reading the memoir of Zhao Ziyang, who was, after the 1989 Tiananmen incident, put under de facto house arrest that lasted for 16 years, the rest of his life. What struck me was, although the press and the world rarely focused on this aspect, this was a case, of course, of administrative detention with no legal authorization. Law reformers generally worry about Chinese citizens losing their freedom for three years under "reeducation through labor." Zhao in effect got a life sentence with no legal process whatever.

Zhao Ziyang was the leader of China. He was Prime Minister. He was the boss. He was head of the Party, and a highly intelligent man who did a lot of good for China. When you read his memoir, you see the reaction of a Chinese leader to a total denial of due process. Zhao never went to law school, but he had no trouble recognizing in his own case that he wasn't given an adequate statement of the charges against him. He wasn't given anyone to advise him, to defend him. He wasn't given an opportunity for the hearing that he kept requesting.

He wasn't given a statement of reasons of why he was being confined in this way and deprived of his rights under the Party Charter, as well as the national Constitution. When it happens to you, even if you're Chinese and the highest leader of the Party, or used to be, you have no trouble seeing a denial of due process of law, of fairness. These are universal values and demands.

When farmers in 1958–1959 had their property taken away from them—kitchen implements, doorknobs, even—so that China could have metal for backyard furnaces to produce steel that was to enable China to overtake England—it was a crazy "Great Leap Forward" idea, of course—they knew, with no education at all, that they had been denied property unfairly. Most Chinese are like most of us when it comes to deprivation of liberty or property.

We should respect China's call for recognition of its many virtues and accomplishments. On the other hand, what kind of a legal system is it going to have? If China's leader's say they will have their own, fine. But what is it, and how fair is it in the eyes of the Chinese people? That is the question that is still before the house 30 years after the initiation of the "open policy."

Ms. OLDHAM-MOORE. Thank you, Mr. Cohen. There's not much else to say after that, except, thank you very much, Bob Fu, Professor James Feinerman, Professor Cohen, and also to our staff person, lead staffer on criminal justice issues, Andrea Worden, who was instrumental in putting this event together, but has a bad case of the flu and could not be present the entire time today.

Thank you for coming. On July 30 the CECC will host another roundtable on press freedom. Jocelyn Ford from the Foreign Correspondents Club in China and her colleagues will be here, so it should be very interesting.

Thank you very much. [Applause].

[Whereupon, at 11:40 a.m. the roundtable was adjourned.]

APPENDIX

PREPARED STATEMENTS

PREPARED STATEMENT OF JEROME A. COHEN

JULY 10, 2009

I am delighted that the Congressional-Executive Commission on China is devoting today's Round Table to a discussion of China's human rights lawyers.

LAW WITHOUT (HUMAN RIGHTS) LAWYERS?

In 1977 Victor H. Li published a stimulating book entitled "Law Without Lawyers." China's Communists, he suggested, because of their country's distinctive tradition and culture, might blaze a new trail toward modernization, one that, unlike their former Soviet model, had little need for lawyers.

Yet Deng Xiaoping and his colleagues soon demonstrated that they thought otherwise. After Chairman Mao's death ended the chaos of the Cultural Revolution, China's new leaders altered the Soviet model for economic development, but resurrected its political-legal system, including its reliance on "socialist lawyers." Indeed, during the past three decades, the post-Mao leadership has increasingly expanded the roles of lawyers to help settle disputes, promote the evolving "socialist market economy," foster international business cooperation and legitimate the punishment of serious offenders.

In principle, contemporary Chinese lawyers are no longer Soviet-style "state legal workers" but independent professionals tasked with protecting citizens, including those at odds with the state. In fact, however, although their numbers, education and responsibilities have burgeoned, Chinese lawyers, like their Soviet predecessors, remain subject to significant restraints.

The Law on Lawyers amended in 2007 seemed to promise greater autonomy to human rights lawyers. Yet their plight has actually worsened in the twenty months since the 17th Communist Party Congress. The reconfirmed Hu Jintao-Wen Jiabao leadership placed veteran Party officials, without legal education or experience but with a strong police background, in charge of the Ministry of Justice and the courts as well as the Central Party Political-Legal Committee that instructs all legal institutions. These new appointees seem determined to eviscerate the country's "rights lawyers," who constitute a tiny fraction—perhaps one percent—of China's almost 150,000 licensed lawyers.

Local officials under the Ministry of Justice, and the local lawyers associations they control, quietly press activist lawyers not to participate in a broad range of "sensitive" matters or at least to follow their "guidance." Such cases include not only criminal prosecutions of alleged Tibetan or Uyghur "separatists," democracy organizers and Falun Gong or "house church" worshipers, but also claims against government for many kinds of misconduct and corruption, birth control abuses and forced eviction and relocation.

Even civil cases involving land transactions, environmental controversies, collective labor disputes and compensation for tainted milk and earthquake victims are off limits or controlled. The refusal to allow famous lawyer Mo Shaoping to defend public intellectual Liu Xiaobo against criminal charges arising from Charter '08's call for political reform is only the best-known recent example of this interference.

Lawyers who fail to heed such "advice" suffer many sanctions.[1] Their license to practice law is frequently suspended or, as in many current instances, their local lawyers association simply fails to give the endorsement required for annual license renewal. Their law firms are coerced to dismiss them or risk being closed, as some have been, and Party organizations within law firms have been reinforced.

Often, ex-lawyers who remain undeterred from assisting controversial clients are prosecuted and sent to prison by authorities who stretch the vague language of criminal law to cover their actions. Unfrocked Beijing lawyer Gao Zhisheng was convicted of "inciting subversion." Former Shanghai lawyer Zheng Enchong served three years for "sending abroad state secrets." Shenzhen lawyer Liu Yao's four-year sentence for "destroying property" was only reduced after an extraordinary petition from over 500 lawyers persuaded the authorities to end his 16-month detention.

In each case conviction means permanent disbarment and loss of livelihood. Moreover, even self-taught "barefoot lawyers," who are not licensed but play an impor-

---

[1] For a selection of essays and materials relating to sanctions against human rights lawyers, see e.g., "Rule of Law," China Rights Forum (No. 1, 2009).

tant role in the countryside, have been sent to long prison terms on trumped-up charges, as in the case of the courageous blind man, Chen Guangcheng.

Perhaps most troubling is the frequent, physical intimidation of "rights lawyers." Today is the 156th day since the "disappearance" of Gao Zhisheng. His torture while previously detained makes many fear that he is now dead, although the Chinese Government ridiculously claims he is free on probation.

Many lawyers, while seeking to meet with clients, have been beaten by police and their thugs. The well-known professor/activist Teng Biao not only lost his license to practice law but also was kidnapped and threatened by police. I can testify from various personal experiences that many "rights lawyers" are closely monitored and restricted in their movements.

Since release from prison, Zheng Enchong's life has been a nightmare of incessant summoning for questioning, illegal house arrest and casual police beatings, in addition to harassment of his wife and daughter. When six policemen barred me from visiting him and I asked for their legal authority, they merely kept repeating "We are police." A sequel to Victor Li's book might appropriately be entitled "Lawlessness Without Lawyers." [2]

THREE RELATED ASPECTS

Before closing, I should mention three other aspects of today's topic that deserve Commission attention.

1. The Relation of Human Rights Lawyers to Political Reform

There has been a difference of opinion among "rights lawyers" concerning the extent to which they should take part in political reform efforts. Some have maintained that, unless China undergoes democratic reforms that eliminate the Communist Party's monopoly of power, prospects for a genuine rule of law will remain dismal. They therefore believe that "rights lawyers" must play an active role in promoting peaceful but major revisions to the political system. Others—a majority so far as one can tell—agree that significant political reform is crucial to achievement of the rule of law but, given the prevailing climate of repression in China, they believe that at present lawyers should dedicate their energies to defending rights within the existing legal system, despite its defects and limitations. This does not preclude working for legislative improvements within the system as well as taking part in individual cases. But it does preclude direct challenges to the Party's monopoly of power.

Among "rights lawyers," the unfortunate Gao Zhisheng was perhaps the leading proponent of opting for political reform. He not only represented Falun Gong and many other controversial clients but also courageously challenged Party rule, condemned the systematic torture of Falun Gong adherents and called for genuine democracy. As a result, as previously indicated, he was deprived of his license to practice law, tortured, convicted of "inciting subversion" and, 156 days ago, "disappeared."

Yet the frustrations confronted by "rights lawyers" occasionally tempt even those who operate within the system to enter the political fray. Many an eyebrow was raised when Mo Shaoping, previously an exemplar of the "professional," non-political view, signed Charter '08's call for political reform.

2. Legal Restrictions on the Professional Conduct of "Rights Lawyers"

Earlier testimony before the Commission has detailed the plight of Chinese criminal defense lawyers. [3] The extent to which the newly-amended Law on Lawyers may have improved the situation remains unclear. Some provisions in the amended Law, which was adopted just before the 17th Party Congress led to enhanced Party controls over the legal system, were designed to strengthen the rights of criminal defense lawyers and their clients. Yet other language in the new Law can easily be manipulated to restrict those rights in fact and to place vigorous lawyers in peril. This is especially true of Article 37, which makes lawyers vulnerable to criminal punishment for courtroom "language that endangers state security" among other things. In the absence of extensive empirical research, which, because of the sensitivity of criminal cases, is difficult even for Chinese scholars to conduct, any assessment of the "law in action" is problematic.

---

[2] The above remarks are a slight expansion of an article that I published in the July 9, 2009 South China Morning Post in Hong Kong and China Times in Taiwan (in Chinese). See www.usasialaw.org.

[3] See, e.g., Jerome A. Cohen, "Law in Political Transitions: Lessons from East Asia and the Road Ahead for China," July 26, 2005, http://www.cecc.gov/pages/hearings/072605/Cohen.php.

Yet even the "law on the books" plainly needs improvement. The Criminal Procedure Law, which last underwent substantial revision in 1996, must be updated to eliminate inconsistencies with the amended Law on Lawyers, and to deal with many long-unresolved issues concerning the lawyer's access to his client and to relevant files, freedom to gather evidence and greater opportunity to participate in the trial. Fundamental questions, such as whether key witnesses should be made to appear at trial and thus be subject to cross-examination, have still not been answered sixty years after establishment of the People's Republic!

Moreover, the formal criminal process is not the only area where "rights lawyers" encounter frustrations. Daily press reports remind us that Chinese police continue to resort to the notorious but supposedly "non-criminal" system of "re-education through labor" (RETL), which authorizes police—without participation of lawyers, prosecutors or judges—to sentence people to as long as three years of imprisonment for a broad range of ill-defined activity. The Ministry of Public Security, in its efforts to beat back proposals before the National People's Congress to abolish RETL, has occasionally experimented with allowing lawyers to take part in RETL proceedings, but generally they are excluded. Usually, the lawyer's only possible role is to assist people who have already been sent off to RETL confinement with an appeal for judicial review in the relatively few cases when the detainees are able to contact and hire counsel. Because China's courts are not allowed to consider challenges to government actions on Constitutional grounds and because the Standing Committee of the National People's Congress has been reluctant to utilize legislatively-authorized procedures for entertaining Constitutional challenges, lawyers have not succeeded in demonstrating RETL's Constitutional flaws.

If the People's Republic should ratify the International Covenant on Civil and Political Rights, which it signed in 1998, that would, at least in principle, expand the role of lawyers in criminal justice and other sensitive matters. As things stand today, however, lawyers are even restricted in their ability to represent the increasing number of groups who need legal assistance in seeking government relief for their grievances and in settling disputes. For example, the 2006 Guiding Opinion of the All China Lawyers Association forbids lawyers from helping groups of ten or more to petition government agencies; and they are required to inform, consult and heed local judicial administration officials and lawyers associations as well as other, unidentified "relevant agencies" regarding cases in which such groups retain them.

3. Licensed Lawyers and "Barefoot Lawyers"

By "barefoot lawyers" I mean laymen, not licensed lawyers, who have informally acquired some legal learning and who apply it, usually in the countryside, in advising people and representing them before courts and other agencies. Until his persecution by the local government in Shandong Province, the blind social activist Chen Guangcheng, now in prison, was a classic and famous "barefoot lawyer." Unable to enlist the help of the few lawyers who practice in rural Yinan County, Chen, who wanted to persuade the county court to order the local government to cease various discriminatory acts against himself and other disabled people, decided to rely on his own efforts. He learned through practice and from several "do it yourself" handbooks on litigation that were read to him by his family.

China has far too few lawyers in the countryside, and some counties have no lawyers at all. Furthermore, some lawyers do not want to take on certain types of cases, whether for financial, political or other reasons. Yet the demand for legal services is rising in the countryside because of economic and social progress and the rising "rights consciousness" among ordinary Chinese that has accompanied this progress. Other important factors are the growing sense of injustice and popular anger against official corruption, plus the government's own propaganda that emphasized ruling the country according to law. Meeting the increasing need for legal services is a huge problem, and "barefoot lawyers" are an understandable, if insufficient, response.

Yet China's legal profession has not uniformly welcomed "barefoot lawyers," fearing that, through incompetence or corruption, they would further sully the reputation of a profession that has experienced difficulty overcoming traditional Chinese distrust and disrespect. Some rural lawyers worry that "barefoot" competition may infringe upon their income. Even some "rights lawyers" who hail from the countryside are wary of relying on "barefoot lawyers."

Until the need for legal services in the countryside has substantially diminished, however, the wiser path would seem to be to offer basic legal training and perhaps certification to the many thousands of "barefoot lawyers" who are urgently required. An experiment worth emulating is the training program organized by Wang Chenguang, former Dean of Tsinghua Law School, with Ford Foundation support. Certainly the issue deserves empirical research and greater attention.

I hope that these brief introductory remarks are useful and look forward to the presentations of my colleagues and the subsequent discussion.

––––––

PREPARED STATEMENT OF JAMES V. FEINERMAN

JULY 10, 2009

This month marks the 30th anniversary of the path-breaking decision of the People's Republic of China (PRC) to turn its back on almost three decades of Maoist antinomian rule and to embrace publicly a new role for law in China's governance. On July 1, 1979, the PRC government promulgated seven new laws—including a criminal code, criminal procedure code and a law on Sino-Foreign Equity Joint Ventures—indicating a new determination to use law in the promotion of the PRC's opening to the outside world and domestic economic reform. Thus it is appropriate that the Congressional-Executive China Commission convene this hearing today to consider the current state of development of China's legal system and the legal profession which serves it.

As members of the Commission already know, China's Communist Party under its current leadership emphasizes building a "harmonious socialist society." One of the stated key components of this project has been enhancing the rule of law. Despite considerable progress over the past almost three decades, China today is hardly a "rule of law" society by Western lights. Unfortunately, for the past several years and even in recent months, activist lawyers, intrepid journalists and those who take on unpopular causes, or represent the disadvantaged and unfortunate, are arrested, intimidated, and silenced. China's nascent bar and weak, poorly trained judiciary offer scant promise of redress.

Why then should we be so concerned with the development of law and the somewhat fitful improvements of the Chinese legal system? Well, from China's perspective, establishing the "rule of law" is critical to China's political stability and further economic growth. We should not forget that this process of legal modernization began on the heels of a devastating, decade-long Great Proletarian Cultural Revolution. This was a time of great disorder in every aspect of Chinese society. The leaders who set China on its current course were, many of them, also victims of the rampant lawlessness and political insanity of that era. So their interest in reform and legality was keen, even if China lacked the usual societal underpinnings for the "rule of law" concept.

If by "rule of law" we mean a system where law restrains state and private power, subjecting even the rulers to its limits, China is still far from realizing such a system. The top leadership—not only in the national and lower-level governments—but more importantly in the all powerful Communist Party are very unlikely to accept such constraints in the foreseeable future. Consistent rules, independent courts and a powerful bar to protect civil and political rights will be a long time coming. Market economy legal rules, on the other hand, have been drafted and put into place much more quickly. Administrative rules to rein in the bureaucracy (and to attempt to force it to follow central government dictates) have been developing apace.[1]

Despite this mixed picture, anyone who (as I did as a participant in the initial student exchange program) saw the reality of China in the late 1970s—when the legal reform developments began—must admit that China has indeed made a "new Long March" from the Maoist era "rule of man" and rampant lawlessness of the Cultural Revolution.[2]

HISTORICAL BACKGROUND

At the famous Third Plenum of the Eleventh Communist Party Congress in December 1978, Deng Xiaoping not only opened China to the world and decreed its economic reform but also called for a rule of law. Since that time, there has been an exponential growth of national legislation, provincial and local lawmaking, and accession to international treaties and institutions. China's entrance to the World Trade Organization (WTO), by itself, required the promulgation of thousands of laws and rules.

Institutions of national scope, such as the National People's Congress (NPC) and its Standing Committee, the State Council, the Supreme People's Procuratorate and

––––––

[1] Jamie P. Horsley, "Rule of Law in China: Incremental Progress," in C. Fred Bergsten, N. Lardy, B. Gill & D. Mitchell, The Balance Sheet in 2007 and Beyond. Center for Strategic and International Studies and The Peterson Institute for International Economics, 2007.

[2] Randall Peerenboom, China's Long March Toward the Rule of Law, Cambridge University Press, 2002.

the Supreme People's Court were either revived or re-established. Over time, they have become much more professional than they were not only thirty years ago but even ten years ago. Throughout China, a small coterie of lawyers and legal reformers promoted legal change and protection of basic rights. Legal aid has become—at least theoretically—available to China's citizens, some of whom avail themselves of such assistance and even make use of the media to assert their rights and try to achieve their objectives even against the government.

Nonetheless, the Communist Party remains in ultimate control; more significantly, the Party and its leadership remain outside the reach of the law, relying upon Party discipline and other mechanisms to maintain a separate superior status. The government bureaucracy—including the courts and other legal institutions—are dominated by Communist Party appointees at every level, despite some autonomy for independent actors to develop the rule of law.[3]

A PRELIMINARY NOTE ON CHINA'S COURTS

Continuing political interference by the Communist Party insures that China's judicial system is far from enjoying the judicial independence that other legal systems take as axiomatic. The implications for legal practice and protection of citizens' rights are ominous. The replacement of the former President of the Supreme People's Court, Xiao Yang, by a man who not only lacks legal training but has long been a Communist Party hack has set back efforts to improve the quality of judges and reform the judiciary. Poorly training and meager compensation of judges leads to corruption which plagues the court system, diminishing its respect and prestige among the Chinese public.

It is also worth noting that China's courts not an independent branch of government. The Standing Committee of the NPC has the final authority to interpret national law. Communist Party adjudication committees inside the courts oversee the work of the judges, particularly in politically sensitive or important cases. Judicial independence is non-existent in China.[4]

WHAT ROLE FOR THE LEGAL PROFESSION?

The modernization of the PRC legal system has required a massive training effort to increase the quantity and the quality of legal professionals. These new lawyers have many roles: to familiarize the general public with the emerging legal system; to draft and to improve the laws themselves; and to serve in government and the private sector as practicing attorneys. Having begun with fewer than a thousand lawyers and less than a dozen law faculties when it began legal modernization in 1979, China now boasts over 130,000 lawyers (with a stated goal of having 150,000 qualified lawyers by 2010) and—depending on how they are counted—anywhere from 400 to 600 law faculties. Compared to the United States and other developed countries, the number of practicing lawyers in China is quite low on a per-population basis, the rapid growth of the bar is remarkable. Many obstacles stand in the way of creating a truly independent legal profession in China. Through the All China Lawyers Association and local-level organizations, PRC lawyers are subjected to Party discipline. The Ministry of Justice and local judicial bureaus exercise strict "supervision and guidance" over practicing lawyers and judges. Nevertheless, a few fearless lawyers and legal scholars have taken courageous positions, often contrary to government and Party dictates, to pushing for legal changes and greater "rule of law" in China.[5]

Along with the increasing number of lawyers, legal education institutions have also mushroomed in China since 1979. While these new faculties have the potential for advancing the "rule of law" in China, many are simply riding a wave of interest rooted in careerism as the profile of law and the legal profession has risen. Law is seen as a lucrative career path for those who pursue certain avenues, as it is in many developed countries. With a hidebound curriculum controlled at the national level by the Ministries of Education and Justice, law schools are usually not too adventurous in training their graduates to consider what might be characterized as "public interest" law. While some, mostly elite, law faculties have introduced clinical legal education, combining hands-on representation of clients with classroom instruction, such programs have had limited impact in communities beyond their immediate environs. A few leading law faculties have also established research centers

---

[3] Xin Ren, Tradition of the Law and Law of the Tradition: Law, State, and Social Control in China, Greenwood Press, 1997.

[4] Benjamin Liebman, China Quarterly, Vol. 191, pp. 620–638 (September 2007).

[5] Gerard J. Clark, "An Introduction to the Legal Profession in China in the Year 2008," Suffolk University Law Review, Vol. 41, p. 833 (2008).

for topics of great public interest—such as worker and consumer rights, women's status in society and the rights of the disabled and disadvantaged—but these programs have so far induced very little change in the larger societal and legal problems facing Chinese society today.[6]

The role of legal academics in the PRC has also been constrained by political realities. While many Chinese legal scholars have studied abroad in countries with more developed legal system, their new ideas about law and legal reform often present a source of controversy in China. Their assistance may be sought in certain narrow areas of legal drafting, but their ideas are often quite suspect when it comes to policymaking. Even when local people's congresses and government legal affairs seek scholars' input, they remain more likely to accept the advice of private law firms and lawyers' associations as more practical. There has been a limited program to employ a few law professors as consultants to governments, but law professors and lawyers are far less likely to work for government agencies than is the case in the United States or other countries. Given the relative lack of legal expertise in most government sectors, and the growing need for legal advice in a society with the stated goal of basing government actions on law, the need for legal professionals to advise the government is obvious. The likelihood that the need will be filled is less certain.

Unlike their counterparts in the United States, Chinese lawyers have very little direct engagement in politics. While a few lawyers serve as local people's congress deputies and on people's political consultative congresses, their impact thus far has been quite limited. Presumably, their legal expertise could help to professionalize the law drafting and other work of these legislative bodies. At the national level, it will be interesting to see whether the ascent of a legally trained leader, Li Keqiang, who is likely to become China's next Premier several years from now will have an impact on the involvement of other lawyers in Chinese political life.

As is true in many other countries, the vast majority of China's law graduates go to work as private lawyers. Nevertheless, a few seek to represent the underrepresented groups in Chinese society. Criminal defendants are supposed to be given legal assistance as a matter of national law. With the assistance of various foreign and domestic organizations (including the United Nations Development Program and the Ford Foundation), legal aid clinics have been sponsored to assist disadvantaged citizens, rural migrants and people with disabilities. Legal aid has become firmly rooted in China's changing legal culture and has helped to raise rights consciousness among sectors of society that have not had much access to the formal legal system in the past. Over a thousand centers have opened in cities across China and are estimated to employ several thousand full-time legal aid workers at a considerable cost to the government. However, these seemingly impressive figures may conceal more than they reveal. Researchers have discovered that these centers often have no real substance and no dedicated employees but rather are often local government offices of the Ministry of Justice with new signage. Moreover, the number of people actually receiving legal aid has not grown at the same rate as expenditures on legal aid which grew more than five-fold from 1999 to 2003, while the number of people receiving legal aid only increased by fifty percent. Despite considerable progress, experts continue to lament the shortage of funds and low access to legal aid.[7]

The reluctance of Chinese lawyers to pursue unconventional areas of practice may be explained by the consequences for those who find themselves in opposition to state and Communist Party. A series of cases over more than a decade have demonstrated that those who undertake criminal defense or politically sensitive cases may face dire consequences. Some criminal defense lawyers have been accused and convicted on trumped up charges of falsifying evidence or committing perjury. Others have been accused of revealing "state secrets"—often nothing more "secret" than newspaper clippings or published maps. This may result in the loss of their jobs and the suspension or cancellation of their licenses to practice law. Just these past few months, the Chinese government has been forcing human rights law firms to shut down. This has not involved a formal crackdown; authorities have not seized files or sent attorneys to labor camps. Instead, the justice authorities are simply using administrative procedures for licensing lawyers and law firms, declining to renew the annual registrations, which expired May 31, of those it deems troublemakers. Human rights groups say dozens of China's best defense attorneys have effectively

[6] Pamela N. Phan, "Clinical Legal Education in China: In Pursuit of a Culture of Law and a Mission of Social Justice," Yale Human Rights and Development Law Journal, Vol. 8, pp. 117–152 (2005).

[7] Xu Jianxin, "Justice and the Need for Legal Aid NGOs in China," China Rights Forum, No. 3, pp. 71–73 (2005).

been disbarred under political pressure.[8] In the time-honored Chinese tradition of "killing the chicken to scare the monkeys," these actions were clearly designed to put the brakes on activism by other individuals and firms.

WHAT HAPPENS TO LAWYERS WHO TAKE ON CONTROVERSIAL CASES AND CLIENTS

The maltreatment of lawyers involved in defending unpopular people and causes is nothing new in China's modern legal system. For years, the Chinese authorities have increased restrictions on lawyers who work on politically sensitive cases or cases that draw attention from the foreign news media. The typical means of harassment is to intimidate lawyers defending criminal defendants by charging them, or threatening to charge them, with various crimes. If that does not work, authorities have also used harassment and violence against those who participate in criminal or civil rights defense in sensitive matters. Detention, house arrest and even imprisonment on manifestly false charges are commonly employed. Pettier forms of harassment have also kept lawyers incommunicado, prevented friends and family members from contacting controversial lawyers and even turned on spouses and children of targeted attorneys.

These practices have excited concern of lawyers elsewhere in the world for the lives and livelihood of Chinese lawyers. In Hong Kong, the China Human Rights Lawyers Concern Group (CHRLCG) made an NGO Submission to the United Nations Committee Against Torture for the 41st session for the Fourth and Fifth Periodic Reports of the People's Republic of China on the Implementation of the Convention Against Torture and Other Cruel, Inhuman or Degrading Treatment or Punishment in October 2008. It noted that although China had ratified the Convention Against Torture and Other Cruel, Inhuman or Degrading Treatment or Punishment (the Convention) in October 1988, dissidents and human rights defenders have continued to be subjected to various forms of torture. In addition to China's failure to effectively implement all the relevant provisions on torture in domestic laws, the report noted, law enforcement officers are usually the ones who violate the domestic laws and the international convention. Recently, CHRLCG became alarmed that the situation was becoming even more worrying because a number of human rights lawyers and legal rights defenders have become the subjects of torture by public security officers and prison officers merely because they provide legal assistance to human rights defenders or took up cases considered "politically sensitive" by the government. Therefore, the CHRLCG expressed concern about how bad the situation is and what problems ordinary Chinese citizens encounter since even lawyers are subjected to torture and harassment by law enforcement officers.[9]

In drawing the Committee's attention to individual cases to illustrate how China has violated the Convention, the CHRLCG noted:

[These] are more well-known cases about mainland Chinese human rights lawyers and legal rights defenders being illegally and unreasonably harassed by law enforcement officers. It is only the tip of the iceberg. There are many more cases involving lesser known human rights legal practitioners. These lawyers were targeted because they took up cases regarded by fellow legal practitioners as highly politically sensitive, such as defending political dissidents, rights defenders and Falun Gong practitioners. Falun Gong is banned in China. These lawyers are only using their professional skills to help people in need. They shouldn't be subjected to oppression and torture by the authorities. If [China] is committed to developing universally accepted principles and the rule of law, it should stop harassing and attacking legal rights defenders and human rights lawyers. Only an independent judiciary and a credible legal system can ensure that these abuses won't happen again. In order to ensure that lawyers, legal rights defenders and ordinary citizens will be free from arbitrary attacks and harassments by law enforcement officers and thugs hired by law enforcement officers, [China] should ensure that law enforcement officers comply with provisions of the Convention.[10]

---

[8] Human Rights in China, "Human Rights Defenders: Harassment and Other Unfavorable Treatment," cited at http://www.hrichina.org/public/contents/press?revision—id=62625&item—id=62623#hrd.

[9] China Human Rights Lawyers Concern Group (CHRLCG), An NGO Submission to the UN Committee Against Torture for the 41st session for the Fourth and Fifth Periodic Reports of the People's Republic of China on the Implementation of the Convention Against Torture and Other Cruel, Inhuman or Degrading Treatment or Punishment , October 2008, accessed at http://www2.ohchr.org/english/bodies/cat/docs/ngos/CHRLCG—China—cat41.pdf.

[10] Id.

With this background in mind, it may be worthwhile to consider briefly a few examples of individual rights defenders in representative cases who have suffered these abuses.

Falun Gong

Human Rights in China (HRIC) has reported on the cases of Beijing rights defense lawyers Zhang Kai and Li Chunfu who were violently beaten at their client's home in Chongqing by local police on May 13, 2009. They were then brought to the local police station for interrogation and were locked up in an iron cage and slapped in the face. A month earlier, Beijing rights defense lawyer Cheng Hai was also violently beaten by the police in Chengdu, Sichuan for handling a Falun Gong case.

Zhang Kai is a lawyer with Beijing Yijia Law Firm and Li Chunfu is a lawyer at Beijing Globe Law Firm. On the afternoon of May 13, they met with relatives of Jiang Xiqing at their home in Jiangjin District, Chongqing to discuss Jiang's death while serving a Reeducation-Through-Labor (RTL) sentence. Jiang Xiqing, 66, was arrested by the police on May 14, 2008, and sentenced to one year of RTL for practicing Falun Gong. On January 28, 2009, the Chongqing Xishanping Reeducation Center informed Jiang's family that Jiang had died of a heart attack. He was then cremated without consent by his family. The family, suspicious of the cause of death, hired a Chongqing lawyer for legal assistance. But after inquiring formally with the police, the lawyer declined to be retained by the family.

Li and Zhang agreed to represent the family, notwithstanding the implied threats experienced when the family had previously tried to retain counsel. Sources inside China informed HRIC that around 4 p.m. on the afternoon of May 13, four policemen came to the home of Jiang's relatives and said they were delivering materials from the public security bureau's judicial administrative office. They started to interrogate the lawyers, asking the lawyers to produce their identity cards. Soon afterwards, about 20 more people from the state security unit of the Jiangjin District Public Security Bureau and Jijiang Police Substation also arrived. Jiangjin State Security squadron leader Mu Chaoheng asked Jiang Xiqing's relatives, "Who told you to hire lawyers? Your dad died a natural death."

After Li Chunfu presented his lawyer's license and Zhang Kai presented his passport, the police announced, "We only accept identity cards." The police surrounded Zhang Kai and Li Chunfu and began pulling their hair, twisting their arms, tripping them, and beating them while pinning them on the ground. The police then handcuffed them and hauled them into their vehicle. They also took away Jiang Xiqing's son, Jiang Hongbin. After arriving at the police station, Zhang Kai was hung up with handcuffs in an iron cage and Li Chunfu was slapped in the face by the police. During the interrogation, the police threatened the lawyer to stop defending Falun Gong cases. When the lawyers argued that everyone had a right to legal counsel, the police said: You absolutely cannot defend Falun Gong; this is the situation in China. Lawyer Zhang Kai later said, "This is typical hoodlum behavior. They just wanted to intimidate us and force us to withdraw from the case. They are so frightened; they must be hiding something about this case."

Zhang Kai and Li Chunfu were released at 12:40 a.m. on May 14. Their hands were covered with bruises and scars. Zhang Kai's hands were numb and swollen, and Li Chunfu had troubling hearing in one ear. Subsequently, they had to be taken to be examined at Jiangjin District People's Hospital.[11]

HIV patients

Hu Jia was a rights defender, not a lawyer, who worked for the rights of those suffering from HIV/ AIDS in rural China. He is the co-founder of the Beijing Aizhixing Institute for Health Education, a non-governmental organization which promotes public awareness and education on the issue of HIV/ AIDS. On March 18, 2008, Hu Jia was tried in the First Beijing Intermediate Court on charges of subversion against the Chinese Government in relation to his on-line writings and has pleaded not guilty. He faced up to five years' imprisonment and is expected to be sentenced in the coming week. Hu Jia's lawyer, Li Fangping, reported that he was allowed only twenty minutes in which to defend Hu Jia and was consistently interrupted by the judge when giving his defense. In addition, several foreign diplomats and members of Hu Jia's family were prevented from attending the trial and many of his supporters were reportedly forced by the authorities to leave Beijing for the duration of the trial in order to prevent them from speaking with journalists.

---

[11] Human Rights in China, "Beijing Lawyers Beaten for Representing Falun Gong Case," May 13, 2009, cited at http://www.hrichina.org/public/contents/press?revision—id=164835&item—id=164831.

Hu Jia was detained on December 27, 2007 after giving his public testimony to the European Parliament in which he gave details of human rights violations reportedly being committed in China. He was officially arrested on January 30, 2008 and charged with "incitement to subvert state power". On April 3, 2008, Hu was sentenced to three years and six months in prison. Hu's wife Zeng Jinyan, after an April 2009 prison visit with Hu Jia, noted that his health is deteriorating because of inadequate nutrition and medical care. Following his arrest his wife, Zeng Jinyan, and his daughter were reportedly prevented from leaving their apartment in Beijing. Several other writers who have published their work on the Internet and are considered cyber-dissidents by the authorities were arrested at the same time.

These arrests have been interpreted as a campaign of intimidation on the part of the authorities against human rights defenders in order to dissuade them from publicizing information about human rights abuses in China during the period of the Olympic Games. Hu Jia has written of human rights abuses committed against those suffering from HIV/ AIDS in rural China, as well as of issues of religious freedom and the human rights situation in Tibet. His lawyer, Li Fangping, a prominent human rights activist, has also been harassed both for representing Hu Jia and for other controversial cases.[12]

Class-action cases

In 2006, the All China Lawyers Association (ACLA) issued a guiding opinion that restricts and subjects to punishment any lawyer who gets involved in a "mass" case. The ACLA Executive Council approved the Guiding Opinion of the All China Lawyers Association Regarding Lawyers Handling Cases of a Mass Nature, which went into effect on March 20, 2006. The following passage, drawn from a translation prepared by the Congressional-Executive Commission on China of the "Guiding Opinion of the All China Lawyers Association Regarding Lawyers Handling Cases of a Mass Nature," distributed by the All China Lawyers Association on March 20, 2006, sets forth the new policy to restrict and inhibit class actions:

> At present and hereafter, during this important era in which our nation is constructing a socialist harmonious society, the correct handling of cases of a mass nature is essential to the construction of a harmonious society. Cases of a mass nature more commonly occur in land requisitioning and levying of taxes, building demolitions, migrant enclaves, enterprise transformation, environmental pollution, and protection of the rights and interests of rural laborers, among other areas. Cases of a mass nature generally have comparatively complicated social, economic, and political causes, and have effects on the state and society that vary in degree and cannot be ignored. Thus, there is a need to standardize and guide lawyer handling of cases of a mass nature.[13]

This Guiding Opinion uses the term "mass" cases to describe those that involve representative or joint litigation by 10 or more litigants, or those in which the matter is handled through a series of litigation and non-litigation efforts. While it notes that mass cases "more commonly occur" in the safeguarding of rights and interests of disadvantaged groups, it clearly seeks to control and to minimize them. Also noteworthy is that the Guiding Opinion instructs law firms to assign only "politically qualified" lawyers to conduct initial intake of these cases, and to obtain the approval of at least three partners before taking them on. Such collective responsibility increases the likelihood that firms will be unwilling to take on these cases. Moreover, lawyers who handle mass cases must "promptly and fully communicate" this information to the local justice bureau, accept supervision and guidance by judicial administration departments, attempt to mitigate conflict, and propose mediation as the method for conflict resolution. Thus, the case will almost certainly never get to court if the tortuous path that the Guiding Opinion sets out is followed. As a final twist, the Guiding Opinion says that local lawyers associations may sanction any lawyer or law firm that fails to follow these guidelines and causes a "negative impact," or report them to the relevant judicial administration department for punishment.

The Guiding Opinion was only one in a series of opinions that restricted the participation of lawyers in specific categories of rights defense work. In addition to "mass" cases, other categories that triggered restrictions included "major," "difficult," and "sensitive" cases. For example, the Henan Provincial Justice Bureau and

---

[12] Human Rights Watch, "Hu Jia Chronology: Key events, February 2006–present," Beijing 2008 China's Olympian Human Rights Challenges, cited at http://china.hrw.org/press/news—release/hu—jia—chronology.

[13] All China Lawyers Association, "Guiding Opinion of the All China Lawyers Association Regarding Lawyers Handling Cases of a Mass Nature," March 20, 2006, English translation available at http://www.cecc.gov/pages/virtualAcad/index.phpd?showsingle=53258.

Shenyang Municipal Justice Bureau (in Liaoning province) each issued opinions governing the range of activities permitted in "sensitive" cases, according to reports in April, 2006.[14]

Tainted food and formula cases

In 2007 and 2008, China was rocked by scandals involving tainted milk and baby formula which poisoned hundreds, causing kidney stones and other medical problems, and even killed a number of children. The products had been adulterated increase its protein count; this in turn revealed a web of corruption and lack of proper oversight in China's food processing industries. A group of 90 lawyers from Hebei, Henan and Shandong—the three worst affected provinces—had made pro bono offers to assist victims, and a list of their names was published. Organizers of the group declared that they had come under pressure from officials to not to get involved in the issue. The Beijing Lawyers' Association, a part of the Communist Party apparatus, asked its members "to put faith in the party and government." Other members of the group reportedly received less subtle requests. Authorities were said to fear social unrest if law suits were unleashed. The Pro-Beijing Hong Kong journal Ta Kung Pao reported that central authorities, fearful of the effect of mass law suits, held a meeting with lawyers' groups in September, 2008, asking them to "act together, and help maintain stability."

Chang Boyang, one of the group of volunteer lawyers, said he had filed a suit in Guangdong against the chief offender, the Sanlu Milk Company, on behalf of the parents of one victim. One had already filed in Henan. Chang said that Henan's justice department had ordered 14 Henan lawyers to stop helping the kidney stone victims, saying it had become a political issue. He claimed he was told by the official to "follow the arrangements set out by the government," and was further threatened: "If this suggestion is disobeyed, the lawyer and the firm will be dealt with." Zhang Yuanxin, lawyer and officer in the Xinjiang Lawyers' Association said that the actions of certain departments in government have "set back the development of the legal profession." He said that it was "intolerable" for government to interfere in the affairs of the judiciary, denying the right of ordinary citizens to sue.[15]

An official said that central government had issued instructions placing the cases on hold, pending a decision on how to handle the cases in a unified manner. Furthermore, that court was instructed not to give any written replies or accept Sanlu-related cases in the meantime.

Sichuan earthquake parents

In the spring of 2008, a terrible earthquake struck China's Sichuan province. Building were leveled, towns destroyed and many citizens killed or injured. Later it was discovered that many of the building were improperly constructed and—had they been built according to applicable regulations—should have withstood the earthquake. Relatives of Sichuan earthquake victims attempted to sue those responsible but became victims yet again. Some were even imprisoned, such as an eight year-old boy who was among those imprisoned by Chinese police attempting to silence protests by the relatives of thousands of children who died in last year's earthquake, according to a new report by Amnesty International. He was held as anger among bereaved parents in Sichuan Province intensified when the authorities went back on their promise to hold a full inquiry into why so many schools were destroyed. The boy was detained overnight last June, along with his father, by police in Shifang City who were looking for his uncle, who had been planning to petition the local authorities over the death of his two sons during the May 12 earthquake.

Roseann Rife, Amnesty's Asia-Pacific Deputy Programme Director, said: "It's absolutely extraordinary that the police would detain a child of that age. It's a violation of the UN Convention on the Rights of the Child, which China has signed up to, as well as Chinese law." Almost five thousand children are known to have died when their schools crumbled to the ground last May in what was the strongest earthquake to hit China in 50 years. Parents of the children have blamed the substandard construction of the schools, many of which collapsed while the buildings around them stayed upright, for the deaths. But officials in Sichuan claim that the

---

[14] See, e.g., "Henan Justice Bureau Establishes a Rule for Lawyers: No Stirring Up of Sensitive Cases"[Henan sifating wei lushi ding "guiju" mingan anjian jin chaozuo], Henan Daily, reprinted in Xinhua (Online), 10 April 06. Cited at <news3.xinhuanet.com>

[15] Edward Wong, "Courts Compound Pain of China's Tainted Milk," New York Times, October 17, 2008, cited at http://www.nytimes.com/2008/10/17/world/asia/17milk.html?ref=asia&p.

force of the earthquake was the primary reason why 9,145 schools in the province were destroyed or damaged.[16]

The government has offered 60,000 Yuan compensation to the parents for each dead child, but only if they agree not to press for an inquiry into the construction of the schools, or to bring court cases seeking damages from the state. According to Amnesty International, an unknown number of those who have petitioned the authorities for an investigation have been detained in unofficial "black jails" for up to 21 days at a time. Lawyers and activists who have assisted them have also been harassed or detained. For example, Luo Guoming claims he was imprisoned for a week last September. His 16 year-old daughter Luo Dan died with another 600 or so children, when the Juyuan Middle School in Dujiangyan collapsed.

"A dozen of us parents were on the way to the provincial capital Chengdu to petition the authorities when the police stopped us and turned us back. The next day, they came to my home and took me away," he said. Mr Luo said he believed his mobile phone was being monitored. He has given up his job as a carpenter to devote his time to seeking justice for his daughter. "I want the authorities to do what they said they would do, which is investigate the construction of the schools, find out who was responsible for such shoddy building work and punish them," he said.

Human rights activists who have offered assistance to the victims, given out information about the earthquake or represented parents in negotiations with authorities have been harassed and arbitrarily detained. Huang Qi was detained because of his work to help the families of five primary school students who died when their school building collapsed during the earthquake. He has been in detention since June 2008, with no access to his family. He Hongchun, a representative of parents whose children died during the earthquake, was detained in September 2009 after he organized a protest outside an insurance company. Tan Zuoren was detained on 28 March 2009, and it is believed that his detention is related to his intention to issue public materials on the first anniversary of the earthquake, including a list of the children who died on 12 May 2008.[17]

CONCLUDING REFLECTIONS AND RECOMMENDATIONS

China's evolving legal system is a substantial change to both long Chinese tradition and the politics and practice of Maoist Chinese political culture. Lawyers and a legal profession are equally new to China and can only become rooted in China slowly. Chinese citizens nonetheless seek ways to obtain redress of governmental abuses of power, to oversee government behavior, and to participate in their society. However reluctantly, the Chinese leadership has decided to foster a growing legal profession and to employ it, suitably constrained, in modernizing China, developing its economy and creating a "harmonious society," with the support of law.

Establishing the rule of law with the help of lawyers is not that easy to control. While welcoming the predictability of legal order, and hoping that legal means can help to curb corruption, China's leaders have already learned that legal activism is difficult to channel. Once ordinary Chinese citizens begin to feel that they have the legal right to courts to enforce their rights, it becomes problematic to tell them that only certain rights warrant protection, especially when those rights are at least theoretically protected by existing laws and regulations.

China's judiciary has thus far served as a lackey for state and Party leaders, heeding their call and accepting the restrictions placed on it. As it becomes stronger, and as lawyers' activism begins to promote judicial independence from government and Party interference, judges may be able to fulfill their roles and reframe Chinese jurisprudence. A more credible Chinese judiciary would also help increase domestic and foreign respect for the Chinese legal system.

The rule of law in China has long been something of an oxymoron, or as Mao used to stress, a "contradiction." The Communist Party remains the final arbiter of not only the rule of law but of all lawful government and refuses subject itself and its minions to the discipline of the law. A professional class of lawyers—well educated, comfortably middle class and increasingly self assured—may eventually be able to wrest greater power over the legal system. And, in contrast to the experience of previous decades, the sunlight of a more active foreign and international press, home-grown human rights defenders (many of them NOT lawyers) and the advantages of modern modes of communication—the cell phone, fax and Internet—assure continued scrutiny of a system about which we know a great deal in detail. That alone

---

[16] Amnesty International, China: Justice denied: Harassment of Sichuan earthquake survivors and activists, May 2009, archived at http://www.amnesty.org/en/library/asset/ASA17/018/2009/en/dbf100fd-c9f7-4675-91b4-e85e25460809/asa170182009eng.pdf.

[17] Id.

may assure continuing pressure to extend the promise of the rule of law to ever larger swathes of Chinese society.

————

PREPARED STATEMENT OF XIQIU "BOB" FU

JULY 10, 2009

Thank you for the invitation to this panel with Professor Jerome Cohen, Professor Feinerman and Mr. Turkel. I very much appreciate the hard work and concern of the CECC Commissioners, including Congressman Pitts who is with us today, and the CECC staff.

I have been receiving many messages from lawyers in China about their law license cancellations or that their licenses have not been renewed by the Beijing Lawyers Association. This is not only unnecessary and unjust, but also an unprecedented development. As far as we can confirm, 19 attorneys at this time are unable to practice law. They are Jiang Tianyong, Li Heping, Li Xiongbing, Li Fuchun, Wang Yajun, Guo Shaofei, Cheng Hai, Tang Jitian, Yang Huiwen, Tong Chaoping, Liu Guitao, Xie Yanyi, Wen Haibo, Liu Wei, Zhang Lihui, Zhang Chengmao, Zhang Xingshui, Wei Liangyue and Sun Wenbing. These attorneys have always persisted in providing legal assistance for clients to safeguard their legitimate rights. Of the reports I have seen, the Open Letter to the Ministry of Justice on July 2nd most succinctly and clearly explains the situation of the license denials and points out the root problems and effects of this on a national level. This letter was written by 31 Chinese intellectuals—23 in Beijing, 7 in other regions of China, and 1 in Australia. I request that the full text of this Open Letter be entered into the Congressional Record. I will read a few key points of the letter:

We think this case is entirely a violation of the law. As a social organization in the legal industry, Beijing Lawyers Association has no right to restrict or deprive its members of their right to practice. In the past, there were cases in which Beijing Lawyers Association deprived some human rights attorneys of their qualifications to practice, and that was considered an illegal overstepping of its authority. Now, it has even forced many law firms to stop their service and made several hundred attorneys unable to practice, which is all the more astonishing. Such illegal, absurd and perverse acts that violate the common sense will bring serious bad consequences to the society.

On July 18, 2008, the Ministry of Justice promulgated "Management Methods in Attorneys' Practice" and "Management Methods on Law Firms" which officially annulled the annual registration system on the attorneys. At this time, Beijing Lawyers Association issued a notice and changed "registration" to "register" and totally disregards the principles of Ministry of Justice in "the specific methods for annual evaluation shall be provided by Ministry of Justice."

. . .First of all, it will further worsen the environment for rule of law in the society. . . . By taking advantage of the authorization from Beijing Bureau of Justice, the Beijing Lawyers Association suppresses and takes revenge on human rights lawyers as it wishes. . . . Most of these attorneys are the topnotch outstanding attorneys who have the highest awareness of rule of law among about ten thousand attorneys in Beijing.

. . .Second, cancellation of the licenses of a large number of attorneys has undermined to a great extent the strategic elements for building a harmonious society.

. . .Third, canceling the right to practice of so many right defense attorneys is a provocation on the social conscience.

The first part of my recommendation for Congressional response is to base the response on this recommendation from the Open Letter to the Ministry of Justice: it is a clear, straightforward framework on which U.S. Congressional response to Beijing can be based. I will read from the Open Letter:

It is our belief that as the highest judicial administrative organ of our country, the Ministry of Justice should not ignore such a violation of law by Beijing Municipal Bureau of Justice and Beijing Lawyers Association in worsening the environment for rule of law, undermining the social harmony and in challenging the social conscience. We hope the Ministry of Justice can, in the principle of "upholding the spirit of rule of law" as proposed at the 17th CPC National Congress, order Beijing Municipal Bureau of Justice and Beijing Lawyers Association to withdraw their decision, correct their mistakes, restore the right defense lawyers' right to practice and apologize to the people in various circles of life, so as to solve this problem in a fair, reasonable and legal way.

I appreciate the clear statements in this letter which explain not only their concern but also the national effects of these license denials—effects which ultimately concern each one of us especially because of the unfortunately utter disregard to rule of law by the largest regime in the world.

One question to be addressed by this panel is, "What is the relationship between these lawyers and the Chinese government and the Communist Party?" This brings up an intriguing point—because these human rights lawyers have been moving forward according to the proposal from the 17th CPC National Congress to "promote the spirit of rule of law" and "realization of rule of law in various jobs of the state." A simple list has been compiled of each lawyer whose license has been revoked or not renewed, and the important incidents and cases the lawyer has been involved with: the categories mentioned in this list include the Sanlu poisonous milk powder incident, abnormal deaths while the victim was in custody, representing house churches, re-education through labor cases, rights of migrant works and ethnic minorities, cases of Falun Gong practitioners, rights of HIV patients, and the case of the underground brick kilns in Shanxi province.

Which of these cases should a government shrink from having represented by a professional lawyer? Does not rule of law necessitate the vulnerability to transparency? Transparency under rule of law, in some of these cases, might necessitate acknowledgement of unjust measures or inappropriate use of authority—and that is unfortunately a consistent possibility in any government because of human nature. What is not necessitated or acceptable is repression of the lawyers who are implementing rule of law.

Not only have human rights lawyers experienced this challenge to their licenses, but some have also experienced actual physical harassment. We have received statements from seven attorneys which I request be entered into the Congressional Record. For example, on May 13, 2009, attorneys Zhang Kai of Kaifa Law Firm in Beijing and Li Chunfu of Globe-Law Lawyers in Beijing were forcibly detained while visiting with a client in a personal residence. They were physically hurt, and thrown in prison for a few hours.

Gao Zhisheng's case continues to baffle and sadden us. He has now been missing for 156 days, since February 4, 2009. The last time he was forcibly taken and hidden in 2007, he experienced 58 days of unspeakable torture. His written account of this torture provides the factual basis for the "FreeGao" DVD available on the table. To date about 100,000 people have signed the online petition at www.FreeGao.com, requesting that accounting be made of Gao's situation and well-being. Why is it that Ambassador Zhou states about Gao that, "The public security authority has not taken any mandatory measure against him?" Why are the officials emboldened to take him, keep him, and refuse to account for him?

Attorney Gao has taken bold stands for freedom and truth in China; he has appealed to the Congress for their support, and it is feared he could be on the verge of death now. Many human rights lawyers in China do not feel they will take the exact approach that Gao has and have made intentional steps to stay generously within the limits of Chinese law—yet, the repression is not even limited to Gao's dramatic moves, but instead we see in the developments with law licenses that even these lawyers' very basis on which to continue work is being threatened.

These developments strengthen the plea to the U.S. Congress to publically investigate these issues, affirm truth and justice, and actively stand for freedom with freedom-fighting, law-loving lawyers in China. Also, I urge the Obama Administration officials and the senior U.S. diplomats in our Embassy in Beijing to publicly, regularly and frequently meet with these freedom fighters in and outside China when they are available so that an unambiguous strong signal can be sent to both these courageous rights defenders and the Chinese government that the American people will stand in firm solidarity with any freedom fighters in any part of the world. Thank you.

SUBMISSIONS FOR THE RECORD

FINAL COMPILATION OF TRANSLATED LAWYERS' STATEMENTS

THE CHALLENGES RIGHTS DEFENSE ATTORNEYS IN CHINA FACE AND ITS FUTURE
PROSPECT

LI FANGPING

July 5, 2009

We are now living in the China set against such a dramatic background of the times: First, the economic system is fast evolving while its political system has seen little changes over the years. Second, its legal system is increasingly improving, but the public power is often not restrained by the law. Third, the citizens' awareness of their rights is increasing and the more the awareness to defend one's rights, the more prominent the abuse and the shirking of responsibilities by the public power becomes.

With the advent of the Internet in China, the first widespread and passionate participation by the citizens in political matters occurred in 2003 during the "Sun Zhigang Incident," which successfully made the State Council announce the annulment of the system of "internment and deportation." In the next year, "The State respects and safeguards human rights" was solemnly written into the Constitution. In the next five years, right defense attorneys have, as a professional social group committed to promoting rule of law and safeguarding human rights, presented themselves before the world.

Certainly, in a country where rule of law is still far from realized and where there is full of terrible things against ordinary citizens, the work and life of right defense attorneys must be full of obstacles and frustrations. Just because we engage in work involving human rights, government departments not only do not understand the significance of our existence, they also regard us as the targets of their domestic defense. We seem to have become personae non gratae in the eyes of the government and we are often treated unfairly. Some of us have been beaten and kidnapped. The personal freedom of some of us is illegally restricted and some of us are illegally stalked by force. Some of us are forced to report our activities and some are driven out by our landlords due to pressure from the government. Some are threatened and given a disciplinary warning by Bureau of Justice and lawyers' associations. Some are simply fired by their law firms due to pressure from the government.

This year, the right defense attorneys as a social group are enduring more pressure than ever before. As far as I can confirm, 19 attorneys at this time are unable to practice law. They are Jiang Tianyong, Li Heping, Li Xiongbing, Li Fuchun, Wang Yajun, Guo Shaofei, Cheng Hai, Tang Jitian, Yang Huiwen, Tong Chaoping, Liu Guitao, Xie Yanyi, Wen Haibo, Liu Wei, Zhang Lihui, Zhang Chengmao, Zhang Xingshui, Wei Liangyue and Sun Wenbing. These attorneys have always persisted in providing legal assistance or defense services for clients to safeguard their legitimate rights. They include victims of Sanlu poisonous milk powder, parents of children victimized in the earthquake, HIV carriers, peasants who have lost their land, detained Tibetans, house church Christians, Falun Gong practitioners, right defense activists, political dissidents, victims of violent family planning policies and clients from other various areas.

Judicial administrative departments in Beijing and other places have terminated attorneys' rights to practice on the ground that these right defense attorneys have not passed the so-called "annual evaluation" or that the law firms where they work have not passed the "annual inspection." However, the "annual evaluation" for attorneys and the "annual inspection" for law firms themselves are not the administrative penalty that can terminate the right to practice of the attorneys or of their law firms. We can see that the "annual evaluation" for attorneys and the "annual inspection" of law firms have degenerated into an illegal, disorderly and remediless administrative penalty in disguised form that overrides the disciplinary penalty in the industry and administrative penalty on the practicing attorneys.

What delights us is that on the one hand, the right defense attorneys have not given up their idea of safeguarding rule of law and human rights. Each time they negotiate with judicial administrative departments, they express their criticism on the illegal administration and their firm belief that China will certainly develop into a country under rule of law. On the other hand, the disadvantaged social groups whose rights are harmed also express their desire of "attorneys for us, and we for attorneys." It is my belief that the appeal for rights by the ordinary people whose rights are harmed, and the sense of mission of the attorneys, will combine to form a powerful synergy in promoting the progress of our country in human rights and rule of law. Though the road to rule of law and human rights in China will be hard and long, yet the long march of this time is attracting more and more people, including you, us and them. Given this situation, I, as a member of this social group of defense attorneys, personally am full of confidence for the "Same World, Same Human Rights."

Finally, let me express my gratitude for all my friends who are concerned about the rule of law in China and the progress in human rights.

* * *

JOINT DECLARATION OF RIGHTS DEFENSE ATTORNEYS

ZHANG KAI AND LI FUCHUN

Night, July 6, 2009

Some of us rights defense attorneys hereby ask ChinaAid Association to publish the following declaration to the international community on our recent sufferings and the worsening prospect for the rule of law in China:

Recently, the rights defense attorneys in China are suffering unprecedented large-scale repression. Rights defense attorneys are a particular social group in China, and they can also be referred to as human rights attorneys. The work the rights defense attorneys do is mainly using the relief of law to safeguard citizens' basic rights within the framework of the Constitution such as freedom of speech, freedom of belief, personal freedom and freedom of property from illegal infringement by the public power, etc. In such a country as China where there is a tradition of thousands of years of autocratic rule and where law is not clearly defined, rights defense attorneys have always been regarded by the authorities as aliens to be expelled and suppressed. Recently, the authorities have become more and more brazen and wanton in such attacks and suppression that the professional licenses of some attorneys were unreasonably rejected during the annual inspection, resulting in their inability to practice their law. A few attorneys were even violently beaten.

The prominent human rights attorneys from Beijing Zhang Kai and Li Chunfu were besieged by over 20 local policemen and met with violence and beatings at the residence of their client when they were in Jiangjin, Chongqing, Sichuan province to investigate the case of Jiang Xiqing who died an abnormal death during custody at a labor camp. Zhang Kai and Li Chunfu were taken away in handcuffs and were detained for six hours. The police illegally examined the computers and the materials the attorneys brought with them as evidence. They tried to force the attorneys to cancel the contract with their clients. As of today, the two attorneys still have not recovered from their injuries. The two attorneys are still trying to talk with relevant departments with reasonable and legal means that they have always used in defending the rights of other people. So far, however, they have not given any official explanations.

We expect the international community to show more concerns on the rights defense attorneys in China. Because the legal system in the Chinese society advances so slowly or even goes backwards, the social conflicts are increasingly intensifying and the ways by which the people seek relief thereof are full of barriers. Given this situation, rights defense attorneys are making great efforts and are paying a great price for the progress of the Chinese law, for which they have made indelible achievements in the history of the progress of rule of law in China. They not only provide legal relief in individual cases, but rights defense attorneys have also played a role in neutralizing social conflicts and in easing tensions between the government and the people. They provide legal assistance and moral support for the miserable Chinese people and are truly promoting the balanced and orderly development of the society.

We also hope the Chinese government can correct its errors in its administration out of its own will and give the rights defense attorneys a legal and sufficient professional environment. Law is the bottomline in guaranteeing that a government wins the support of its people. It is also the last line of defense with which the people can enjoy the freedom and safety in their life. They should give the rights defense attorneys more encouragement and support, not suppression or injury. Otherwise, such an injury can affect the image and dignity of the Chinese government itself.

Doubtlessly, every human being created in the image of God the Creator enjoys the rights of freedom and equality. The Constitution is the reality of protection of such rights which no one or no government has the right to deprive the people of. This type of rights is natural and has universal values. Rights defense attorneys adhere to the basic spirit endowed by the law and plead on behalf of the people for freedom and equality. And such rights originated from the authorization of God and transcend all countries and races, whether they are Chinese, Americans or tribes in Africa. When man's rights and dignity are hurt, it is the loss on the glory of the Creator. Every one of us has the obligation to strive for improvement on this issue. We hope there will be changes in the Chinese society and we are willing make our efforts in building a free and democratic country under rule of law based on the law of China and the spirit endowed by the law.

Zhang Kai, attorney (Yijia Law Firm of Beijing)
Li Fuchun, attorney.

* * *

HUMAN RIGHTS ATTORNEYS IN CHINA VERY ACTIVE BUT FIND THEMSELVES IN A DIRE SITUATION

JIANG TIANYONG

Since 2005, the social conflicts in China have been intensifying, but people are fast awakening in the awareness of their rights. Given such a background, the rise of the right defense movement has produced a group of human rights defenders such as Gao Zhisheng, Chen Guangchen, Guo Feixiong, Hu Jia, Li Heping, etc. Human rights attorneys are an important group of these people. The human rights attorneys in China work in a wide range of fields such as the freedom of religious belief, freedom of speech, freedom of association, residential rights (objection to forced removal), land rights, rights of ethnic minorities (such as Tibetans), etc. On the one hand, they are becoming more and more active and are more and more needed and depended upon by victims whose human rights are abused. On the other hand, they suffer harassment, repression and persecution from the government.

Following is my experience to demonstrate this situation:

My name is Jiang Tianyong, and I'm a male of Han nationality. I was born in Henan province, PRC in 1971. Currently, I'm residing in the Haidian District of Beijing, China. Because I wanted to engage in work of defending human rights, I quit my work at a middle school in Henan province and came to work at Beijing Globelaw Firm in 2004. In 2005, I got my attorney's license and became a practicing attorney. After that, I've taken a large number of human rights cases, both individually or in partnership with my associates. As a result of this, I've suffered various forms of persecution from the government. Except 2007, I met troubles in renewing my attorney's license at Beijing Bureau of Justice during the annual inspection/registration/annual evaluation in 2006, 2008 and 2009.

In 2006, as I was involved in right defenses cases of migrant workers, Gao Zhisheng's case, victims of violent family planning policies in Linyi, Chen Guangchen's case, I was harassed and threatened by the secret police of Domestic Security Protection Squad of Beijing. They tried to prevent me from participating in these so-called sensitive cases, claiming that it was not good for me. They also said that if I wanted to make a fortune, they could help. Their demands were not unfulfilled. People from Beijing Municipal Bureau of Justice found me through my law firm and told me they forbad me to get involved in some cases. They even used special means in getting to know that I had bought a train ticket to go to Linyi for the violent family planning case. They called me many times and forbad me from going there. Even my wife who was living far away in Zhengzhou, Henan province was harassed on the phone by them in the middle of the night. In the meantime, as my landlord could not endure the pressure from the secret police, and he refused to continue renting the house to me. I had to move out. In the same year, the registration of my attorney's license and Li Heping's license got into trouble and were delayed. Beijing Municipal Bureau of Justice illegally forced me and my law firm to write a statement of guarantees.

Starting from August 2006, I was illegally stalked because of Gao Zhisheng's case and was placed on house arrest for five months.

In 2008, I continued engaging in cases of human rights and began to provide legal assistance to people sentenced to re-education through labor and HIV carriers. I also provided legal support for NGO organizations that defend human rights—for example, Aizhi Research Institute of Beijing (www.aizhi.net) and Open Constitution Initiative (OCI) (www.gongmeng.cn). After the March 14 Incident in Tibet, I signed a declaration to express my willingness to represent the arrested Tibetans. In that year, I met with serious troubles from Beijing Municipal Bureau of Justice during the annual inspection and registration of my attorney's license. They unequivocally told me the reason: "You have gotten involved in sensitive cases." They said they wanted to "unleash their wisdom" and "break the livelihood" of us human rights attorneys. Beijing Municipal Bureau of Justice tried illegally to force me to write a statement of guarantees in which I would promise not to get involved in sensitive cases again and not to have interviews with the media. Because their demands lack legal basis, they were rejected by me. After widespread concerns from people both in China and abroad, I finally passed the annual inspection and registration on June 30 of that year. At this time, I have not been able to engage in attorney's work for a month now.

From July 2008 to May 2009, I represented a large number of people in cases ranging from Falun Gong, HIV carriers in defending their rights, earthquake victims (such as Hong Chun case), Tibetans (such as Phurbu Tsering Rinpoche the living Buddha and Jigma Lama). I also participated in the direct election of Beijing Lawyers Association. Because of this, I was seriously persecuted by Beijing Municipal Bureau of Justice and Beijing Lawyers Association. They joined forces in trying to force the law firm where I worked not to renew our contract. From the end of 2008 to March 2009, the head of Globe-Law Lawyers where I worked talked with me on many occasions and told me that "since we work under them, we have to yield." "We really can't endure the pressure from the above (referring to Bureau of Justice and Beijing Lawyers Association) and "We shouldn't be closed (by Beijing Municipal Bureau of Justice and Beijing Lawyers Association) just because of you (representing people in cases involving human rights), etc." In the 2009 "Annual Evaluation" of attorneys, the great majority of Chinese human rights attorneys who strictly adhere to law have failed to pass. Six human rights attorneys from our law firm are all among these attorneys who have failed to pass. They are myself, Li Heping, Li Xiongbing, Li Fuchun, Wang Yajun and Guo Shaofei. May 31, 2009, the expiration date for the annual evaluation and we haven't been able to engage in jobs as an attorney since then. Now, we not only can't accept new human right cases, but we also have to stop on cases that we have already accepted before this date, such as the case of Li Zhigang of Shenyang (Falun Gong), He Hongchun case (a case from the earthquake disaster areas), the case of Phurbu Tsering Rinpoche (case involving Tibetan issues) and other human rights cases. When human rights attorneys themselves are bogged down in a difficult situation, the rights of the clients in human rights cases also lose their protection instantly! Other human rights attorneys and I myself have made inquiries at the relevant people at Beijing Municipal Bureau of Justice and Beijing Lawyers Association, but nobody has given us an official reply. So far, we still have not received any documents in writing related to the result of our annual evaluation results. Yet, the hints we have received from Beijing Municipal Bureau of Justice, Beijing Lawyers Association and our own law firm show that our current predicament has something to do with the cases we have accepted. At about 11:20 a.m. on July 3, Attorney Zhang Xuebing, president of Beijing Lawyers Association told us in the capacity as an "attorney of our own kind":

"I know something about your issues. This issue is actually very complicated. As the old saying goes: 'Rome was not built in a day. Doubtlessly, every human being enjoys the rights of freedom and equality because of the creation by God' and it is not that easy to solve this problem. You'd better talk with your superiors, and I'm afraid you still have to find a way to win the trust of the Party and the government!'"

Starting from 2006, I have always been placed on house arrest on June 4 anniversaries, October 1, the Beijing Olympics and state visits by important diplomats (including China—Africa Forum on Cooperation, visit in 2008 by Congressmen Wolf and Smith). Though I was in America when U.S. Secretary of State Hillary Clinton visited China, my family was harassed on many occasions by the police. From June 3 to June 7 of 2009, the police were deployed at my door and prohibited me from leaving the house. They threatened me with my personal safety and the safety of my wife and my daughter.

No matter how we suffer, we the human rights attorneys will still adhere to our own belief and will never give up our efforts in winning and defending human rights. In the meantime, we also call on the people who live in the free world and under rule of law to show concern to the efforts made by Chinese people in winning and defending human rights. This is because as long as there are still members of the human race who live in fears and lack of freedom, the enjoyment of freedom and human rights is very likely to be short-lived.

* * *

FIGHTING FOR RIGHTS CONTINUES EVEN AS PERSECUTION ESCALATES—A HUMAN RIGHTS ATTORNEY'S EXPERIENCE AND PERSEVERANCE

TANG JITIAN

My name is Tang Jitian. I am male of Han nationality. I was born in Jilin, China, on September 1, 1968. I am currently residing in Chaoyang District, Beijing Municipality, China. I started practicing law in 2005 and relocated from Guangdong to practice law in Beijing in 2007. I am now a practicing attorney with Anhui Law Firm of Beijing.

Since August 2008, my normal law practice has been seriously interrupted. At the beginning, I was notified several times by my former law firm (Beijing Haodong Law Firm) that my contract would be terminated ahead of schedule or I should cease my practice. The reason was that the Beijing Municipal Judicial Bureau and Beijing Lawyers Association were infuriated by my and other colleagues' call for direct election of Beijing Lawyers Association. I found my current law firm before my contract of employment expired, but during the course of transfer, my case was unreasonably delayed for nearly twenty days by the judicial administrative department and Beijing Lawyers Association. (The processing clerk said in private that the same thing happened to all those on the blacklist.) Since June 2009, the government has again, in a disguised form, deprived me of my right to practice law. But I have not committed any violation of law or regulations. And my work as an attorney has never been criticized or complained about by my clients. On the contrary, many people, including my clients, often spoke to me directly or on the phone or in their letters about my work, praising me for defending human rights in accordance with law. They encouraged me to overcome the pressure and oppression from the government by giving me their support. They, of course, also felt worried about my situation.

The reason I was suppressed and persecuted by the government is that as an attorney I was involved in quite a lot of work defending human rights. About a week before I was forced to stop practicing law, a police officer named Wang from the General Domestic Security Protection Squad of Beijing Municipal Public Security Bureau called to make an appointment for a talk with me. His demand was rejected by me. (In April, Wang, together with Sun Di, head of the Domestic Security Department and a police officer surnamed Han, had already talked with me regarding the issues such as Charter 08, representation of cases, and the direct election of Beijing Lawyers Association.) After that, Sun Di again called me, demanding that we have a talk. After he was rejected by me, he threatened me by saying that he could find me through other methods.

Soon afterwards, after six o'clock on the morning of June 3, 2009, under the pretext that we needed to cooperate with an investigation of a case of so-called burglary that had taken place, Attorney Lan Zhixue and I were first prohibited from going out freely. Then we were taken to the Sijiqing Police Station in Haidian District, Beijing Municipality. After they had interrogated me and taken a written record, the police officers at that station unreasonably and illegally detained me till eight o'clock in the evening. That night when I was on my way back to my residence, I was followed and stalked by police officers Lu Yonghui and Zhang Jian from the Domestic Security Protection Squad of Public Security Branch of Haidian District, Beijing Municipality as well as police officers Li Jing and Shi from Sijiqing Police Station. This continued till dawn on the 4th. Later, these police officers sent for additional police officers. Blocking attorney Dong Qianyong, who was with me, they forcibly pushed me into the car and drove me to their secret detention spot. (It is now known that this place is called Kao Fu Te Sports Training Center and is in the vicinity of the Linglong Bridge in Haidian District.) In the few days that followed, they arranged police officers and security guards to keep watch over me, forbidding me to contact the outside world. Furthermore, I was not allowed to step out of the room at all. During my detention, Lu Yonghui from the Domestic Security Protection Squad and the police officer named He who later joined him held several rounds of what they called exchange of communications, asking me not to get involved with human rights cases (such as the cases of Falun Gong), and not to demand rights from the Judicial Bureau and the Lawyers Association, and not to take part in any social affairs that will irk the government. They stated several times that if I did not cooperate, I could have trouble living and working in Beijing. On June 6, I was transferred to a hotel (I later learned that it was called Dong Lun Xin Xing Hotel) in Chaoyang District where I was held in custody till the evening of June 7 when I regained my freedom. In the past few days, at the request of the police, the owner of the house that I have been renting has asked me to move out and relocate somewhere else.

Over the past few years, as an attorney I have been mainly engaged in defending citizens' right to freedom of expression, right to freedom of religion, right to housing, right to land, and other fields of human rights. It is exactly for these works that I was repudiated and treated with hostility by the government. These works include legal defense for persecuted believers such as Falun Gong practitioners, representation of Wang Zhaojun whose right to freedom of speech and expression was infringed upon by Sina.com (Wang's blog site was shut down by Sina.com because he published "A Letter to the Chinese People"), and advocacy of the rights of the farmers who have lost their land as well as advocacy of the right to equal employment.

With regard to defending our own rights as attorneys, my efforts focusing on pushing for direct election of Beijing Lawyers Association have also become one of the major reasons why some officials have identified me as a "non-mainstream" attorney.

Since April 2009, making illegal use of the annual evaluation, Beijing Municipal Bureau of Justice and Beijing Lawyers Association have instructed the Judicial Bureau of Chongwen District several times to have the law firm under its jurisdiction fire me, stating that if attorneys like me were not fired, then the law firm would be subject to rectification and reform indefinitely.

As of today, there has been no change whatsoever in my situation where the government, by subjecting me to an illegal annual evaluation, has in a disguised form, deprived me of my right to practice law.

* * *

PRACTICING LAW UNDER UBIQUITOUS PRESSURE

LI XIONGBING

My name is Li Xiongbing, and I am male of Han nationality. I was born in Hubei, China, on September 18, 1973, and I'm currently residing in Tongzhou District, Beijing Municipality, People's Republic of China. Since 2005 I have been working as a practicing attorney at Beijing Globe-Law Firm.

After the registration of my attorney license was postponed in 2008 by Beijing Municipal Bureau of Justice on the grounds that I had "handled sensitive cases," my qualification as an attorney and my right to practice law has again been arbitrarily revoked by Beijing Municipal Bureau of Justice since June 2009. However, I have never committed any violations of law or regulations, and my work as an attorney has never been blamed or criticized by my clients. On the contrary, many of my clients and members of the general public often call me or write to me to praise my work, encouraging me to overcome the pressure from public powers and become an outstanding human rights attorney.

The frequent suppression and persecution I have suffered while working as an attorney are directly linked with my advocacy for human rights. Precisely on the morning of May 31, 2009, the day when my work as an attorney was about to be illegally terminated, two police officers from Domestic Security Protection Squad from the Beijing Municipal Public Security Bureau made an appointment to talk with me. They expressly gave me two warnings. First, that I should not defend Falun Gong practitioners ever again. Second, that I should not participate again in the relevant work of a non-governmental organization dedicated to pushing for the rule of law and human rights progress. I persisted in practicing my profession independently in accordance with law and rejected their unreasonable demands.

As expected, soon afterwards, I failed to pass the annual evaluation for my attorney license, and I was unable to practice law. Starting from June 2, I was monitored and followed by police officers or police cars for eight days in a row and was not allowed to go to any place without prior approval from the police and meet with anyone without prior approval of the police. It was not until the evening of June 9 that I regained my freedom. In addition, on the evening of June 5, at the request of the police, the owner of the house that I was renting came to my home, asking us to move out and leave Beijing. The kindergarten my child was attending was also harassed by the police and had to relocate to a place far away from my residence. My pregnant wife was also questioned and investigated several times by the relevant departments due to her lack of a so-called "pregnancy permit" and, she received warnings and threats.

Over the past few years, my work as an attorney has been mainly concentrated on these areas: advocacy of civil rights such as citizens' right to freedom of expression, the right to freedom of religion, and equal rights as well as public legal services. It is exactly for the work in these areas that I was repudiated and treated with hostility by the government. My work includes the case of Qi Chonghuai, a journalist for Legal Times, involving the freedom of speech; the case of Yuan Xianchen, a human rights worker in Heilongjiang province, involving instigation of the subversion of the government; the case of providing legal assistance to victims of Sanlu poisonous milk powder; the case of providing legal assistance to victims of child slavery in "illegal brick kilns" in Shanxi, as well as legal defense cases involving religious persecution of believers such as those of "Falun Gong" and the faction of "Three Grades of Servants."

At the end of 2008, because I provided legal assistance to the victims of toxic Sanlu milk powder, I was warned and threatened several times by Beijing Municipal Bureau of Justice, Beijing Lawyers Association, and other departments. In the summer of 2008, I was also suppressed and threatened several times by Beijing Municipal Bureau of Justice, because I had provided legal assistance to the families of children victimized in the earthquake disaster area, and was forced to stop providing legal aid.

As recently as the morning of June 30, 2009, Huang Weizhong, a believer of Falun Gong in Jiamusi Municipality of Heilongjiang Province, was detained and tried. I took the case in April 2009 and acted as a defense attorney for Huang Weizhong. However, when the court trial started on the morning of June 30, the People's Court in the suburbs of Jiamusi Municipality blocked me from entering the court to perform my job as an attorney on the grounds that I failed to pass the annual evaluation Beijing Municipal Bureau of Justice. Without having me present as his defense attorney, Huang Weizhong was sentenced to three years of imprisonment.

* * *

Defending Rights in Hardship and on a Thin Line

Wen Haibo

Personal resume: Wen Haibo is a male of Han nationality. He was born in Liaoning, People's Republic of China in 1980. Currently, he resides in Chaoyang District, Beijing Municipality, PR China. He started his career as an attorney in 2004 and once worked at Shengzhi Law Office and Yitong Law Firm. Currently, he is a practicing attorney in Shunhe Law Firm of Beijing.

From November 2005 to March 2009, Shengzhi Law Office and Yitong Law Firm, both places where I once worked, were given administrative penalties of "suspending business for reorganization" due to different but groundless reasons given by judicial authorities of Beijing. The true reasons were none other than that these law firms had gotten involved with or had participated in some cases and incidents with which the authorities were not pleased.

I started working with Attorney Gao Zhisheng in April 2004 until the law firm was shut down in November 2005, and I was forced to leave. During this time, both Attorney Gao and I represented a large number of people from socially disadvantaged groups in defending their rights. When we began to defend the rights of Falun Gong adherents in 2005, the suppression we suffered escalated gradually. At first, the judicial authorities or the people working in Beijing Lawyers Association constantly made appointments with us for talks where they gave us a warning of "not allowing you to accept Falun Gong cases." After that, the police constantly harassed, stalked us and videotaped us without permission. At the end of 2005, after Attorney Gao launched a campaign of "hunger strike to fight against violence," I and several other people working in the law firm were one by one placed under house arrest. When I was under house arrest,, several plainclothes policemen stayed downstairs 24 hours a day, and they did not allow me to go out. When I had to go out (such as for shopping), someone shadowed me closely. This lasted 45 days.

I left Shengzhi Law Office at the end of 2005 and went to work at Yitong Law Firm. During this time, besides defending the rights of Falun Gong adherents, I also signed in with the attorneys' delegation to provide legal assistance for the Tibetans arrested during the March 14 Incident in Tibet. The signatures for that delegation brought such a great repercussion that about 10 attorneys who joined the delegation all received warnings from the judicial authorities and the police. The police station in charge of my area also made an appointment with me for a talk. They threatened me and told me to leave Beijing. I flatly refused. In the second half of 2008, I also joined the movement of calling for "the direct election of Beijing Lawyers Association." The mention of "direct election" obviously touched the frail nerves of some people in the judicial departments. They counterattacked in a high profile way, and denouncing us as "linking up with each other in private, using democratic election as a signpost, publishing seditious remarks, spreading rumors among the lawyers in Beijing to bewitch the people," "attempting to break away from the supervision and guidance of the judicial administrative departments and the administration of the Lawyers Association in order to deny full-scale the current administrative system on attorneys, the judicial system and even the political system."

As many attorneys from Yitong Law Firm joined in calling for "direct election," the judicial authorities intended to "kill one as a warning to many others" and suspended Yitong Law Firm for reorganization.

When Yitong Law Firm was shut down at the end of 2008, I was again forced to transfer, this time to Shunhe Law Firm. Since I did not stop getting involved in various cases of human rights and mass groups defending their rights, I brought suppression here, too. Since I did not pass the annual evaluation by Beijing Lawyers Association, I cannot practice normally at this time, and several cases I have accepted before were forced to stop.

Though I have met temporary (possibly long-term or permanent) difficulties in my work, I have received the encouragement and support from my clients and other friends. With this encouragement and support, I do not feel lonely and will continue walking along this road!

○

www.ingramcontent.com/pod-product-compliance
Lightning Source LLC
Chambersburg PA
CBHW080108010626
45794CB00015B/3318